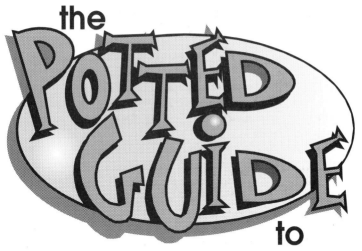

the POTTED GUIDE

to THEOLOGY

WHAT DOES THAT MEAN?

DUNNO.

paternost
press

D0271100

This delightful book is a remarkable achievement. In an accessible way it accurately distils the complex thoughts of the great and famous. Anyone wanting a way into theology ought to read this book.
Professor Ian Markham, Professor of Theology and Public Life, Liverpool Hope University.

Tony Gray's anatomy of Christian theology is deft and wise. Laughing brings the giants of theology – an aspect of human learning not well-known for its humour – down to size. What is more important, laughing helps learning. So this book is sure to be a tonic for any theological faintheart.
Professor Paul Helm, King's College, London.

I didn't think it could be done, but it is great fun, and informative, too.
Keith Ward, Regius Professor of Divinity, University of Oxford.

How can you grapple with vital issues in the history of the Christian faith and not get bored or confused? Read the **Potted Guide to Theology**.
Nigel Lee, Head of Student Ministries, UCCF.

the POTED GUIDE to THEOLOGY

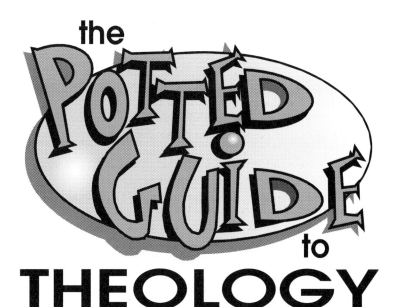

TONY and STEVE
GRAY ENGLISH

First Published 2000 by Paternoster Press

06 05 04 03 02 01 00   7 6 5 4 3 2 1

Paternoster Press is an imprint of Paternoster Publishing,
PO Box 300, Carlisle, Cumbria, CA3 0QS, UK
and Paternoster Publishing USA
Box 1047, Waynesboro, GA 30830-2047
www.paternoster-publishing.com

British Library Cataloguing in Publication Data

A catalogue record for this book is available
from the British Library

ISBN 0-85364-916-2

Cover design by Steve English
Printed in Great Britain by
Bell & Bain Ltd., Glasgow

CONTENTS

INTRODUCTION

WHAT IS THEOLOGY?

What is an "ology"? Even worse, what sense can we make of **theology**? Theology used to be known as "the queen of the sciences".

Science as we know it today examines life, the universe, how it works, and where human beings fit in.

That's exactly what theology looks at, from a different angle. Theology looks at the BIG QUESTIONS of life.

IS THERE A PURPOSE TO LIFE

DOES GOD EXIST

WHY AM I HERE

WHO WAS JESUS AND DOES IT MATTER

WHY IS NAVEL FLUFF ALWAYS BLUE

2

The word "theology" can seem bizarre and boring. It comes from two Greek words -

theos and **logos**
for **God**   for **word**.

So theology is concerned with words and thoughts about God. All those big questions are tied up with thinking about God, or rather, with theology. Theology can have a whole range of meanings, and applications.

Theology can be done in church, or at university.

It can be done by brilliant intellectual professors,

or by everyday lay people.

It can try to work out what the very nature of God is,

or it can ponder about the best way to pray.

It can involve technical philosophy, or the simplest meditations. And, casting our theological net further, it can involve discussion of one religion, traditionally Christianity, or a whole range of religions. This potted guide takes you through **Christian** theology, past the different men (and some women - that's an issue for feminist theology, see later!) that make up the story of Christian theology.

3

WHEN DO WE

Theology may be something you never intended doing. However, school, church, university - these are not the only places for theological thinking.

HAVE YOU EVER SAT AT THE EDGE OF THE OCEAN, WITH THE VASTNESS AND THE COMPLEXITY OF THE UNIVERSE RUSHING IN AT YOUR FEET, AND BEGAN TO PONDER WHAT THE MEANING OF LIFE IS?

OR HAVE YOU EVER HAD ANYONE TRY TO TELL YOU WHAT THEY BELIEVE ABOUT GOD - EVEN IF THEY SEEMED A BIT ODD, WHAT SHOULD YOUR VIEW BE?

HELLO, CAN I TELL YOU ABOUT...

So much of the world around us is influenced by religion and theology.

Conflict in Northern Ireland,

how states and governments are run,

PRESIDENT

when we are allowed to go shopping,

and whether we should listen to our horoscopes .

Theology has much to say about all these. So, theology is not restricted to one particular time or place. As this book hopes to show you, theology touches on issues which everyone will one day think about.

HOW DO WE DO THEOLOGY?

For centuries theologians have argued about how to do theology - after all, talking about God is a bit more complicated than talking about the weather!

NICE GOD WE'RE HAVING!

I BELIEVE HE'S GOING TO TURN WINDY TOMORROW!

Do we just sit down and think?

Do we blindly obey all that a particular church teaches?

What about the things we feel - do they have a part to play in how we do theology?

Is reading and following the Bible the simplest way to do theology, forgetting everything else?

Throughout Christian history, various people have adopted different models on how to do theology. What matters most are the different *sources* from which people make claims, and what *authority* these sources have.

Think about the claim that God created the world. Why believe such a thing?

One person will take *revelation* as their authority, believing that God as a creator is taught in the Bible, and that the revelation of Jesus confirms this.

Another will believe in God as creator because their priest taught them this in Sunday school - so they take *tradition* as their authority.

Maybe someone experiences something miraculous - although blind since birth, now they can see! Who could blame them for relying on their *experience* to claim that God has the power to create?

A fourth person may believe in God as creator because of something much more 'reasonable'. Looking around at the complexity of the universe, they use their *reason* to conclude that this world results from creation, not just blind chance.

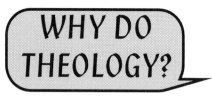

WHY DO THEOLOGY?

Having heard all of this, one last question may remain. Why bother with theology at all?

LEAVE ME OUT OF IT, AND LET ME GET ON WITH MY LIFE.

But think of some of the things looked at already. Think of those big questions, and the way they can change our lives. If God does exist, and he is concerned about us, then think what could change -

what job you take,

how you use your money,

what you drink at the pub,

who you vote for,

who you might marry, and so on.

So, if studying theology changes all these things, then it is terribly important.

8

On the other hand, if you decide religion has no point, then at least you have looked, and may know something of what everyone else is on about.

AT LEAST WHAT YOU NOW DECIDE IS BASED ON INFORMATION, NOT GOSSIP AND HEARSAY.

If you are a Christian, you may at times find studying theology difficult. It can raise questions and difficulties that you never came across before.

However, if this book goes some way to helping you understand...

WHAT you believe **AND** **WHY** you believe it,

maybe it can help your faith to have an even deeper impact on your life...

This last question, **WHY STUDY THEOLOGY?** brings us back to the **WHAT** of theology. For, if theology is asking big questions, then asking **WHY DO THEOLOGY?** may be one of those questions. So the very answer to that question may lie in...

DOING SOME THEOLOGY...

9

A GUIDE TO THE

You will probably want to use this book for reference purposes, and so we have created a few pointers to help you find your way round the book without having to read from page to page.

Each chapter will focus on the theologians of that period, and each theologian can be identified by a mug shot (pretty ugly at that some of them) along with their name.

MAINLY THESE WILL BE FOUND AT THE TOP OF THE PAGE AND THE TEXT THAT FOLLOWS WILL GIVE A SMALL INTRODUCTION TO WHO THEY ARE.

THIS ICON WILL INDICATE WHEN THE TEXT IS ON ABOUT A PARTICULAR THEOLOGIAN'S THEOLOGY. SO LOOK OUT FOR THIS TO FIND OUT WHAT THEY THOUGHT ABOUT AND BELIEVED IN.

To help you understand how the story of theology fits in with the rest of history a time-line runs through the book highlighting some milestone events from the past.

Had breakfast.	Went to the toilet.	Ate my dinner in two minutes flat.
1725	1733	1745

THE PATRISTIC PERIOD

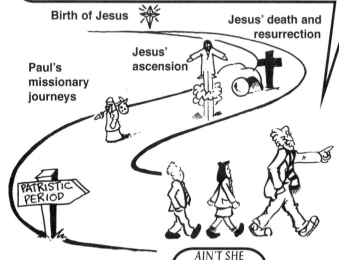

AFTER THE PERIOD OF THE NEW TESTAMENT, CHRISTIAN THEOLOGY BEGAN TO GROW AND DEVELOP AS IT REFLECTED ON THE EARLY CHURCH'S EXPERIENCE, AND ADDRESSED THE QUESTIONS OF THE DAY.

Birth of Jesus

Jesus' death and resurrection

Jesus' ascension

Paul's missionary journeys

PATRISTIC PERIOD

This first part of Christian history is known as the PATRISTIC PERIOD, named after the 'fathers' (Latin, *patres*) of the church who were the first theologians. These theologians are often appealed to as authorities by later thinkers, and they struggled with a whole range of issues.

AIN'T SHE GREAT?

WAAH WAAH

Their theology was not dry and abstract. It was developed as a result of their worship which caused them to think about some of the most important doctrines of the church for the first time. They thought deeply about issues of -

TRADITION

AUTHORITY

NATURE AND EXTENT OF THE *CANON* (RULE) OF SCRIPTURE

Although their culture and language may seem abstract, for them it was deeply relevant, often worth laying down their lives for.

14

The early church began because it started to proclaim Jesus Christ as Lord. The impact of this is seen in their discussions about who and what Jesus was (discussions of the nature and person of Christ, traditionally called *Christology*). How could Jesus be both divine and human at the same time, as they claimed? In turn, this led to questions about the nature of God, and the doctrine of the *Trinity*.

Other issues debated included...

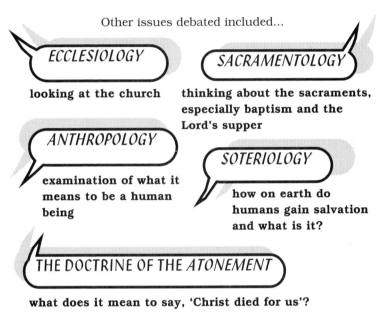

ECCLESIOLOGY

looking at the church

SACRAMENTOLOGY

thinking about the sacraments, especially baptism and the Lord's supper

ANTHROPOLOGY

examination of what it means to be a human being

SOTERIOLOGY

how on earth do humans gain salvation and what is it?

THE DOCTRINE OF THE *ATONEMENT*

what does it mean to say, 'Christ died for us'?

THE PATRISTIC PERIOD IS FULL OF FASCINATING CHARACTERS, DEBATES, POLITICS, MARTYRS AND MORE. NOT ONLY IS IT AN INTERESTING PIECE OF HISTORY, BUT IT IS FOUNDATIONAL AS THE BUILDING BLOCK FOR THE REST OF CHRISTIAN THEOLOGY.

FOR QUITE A FEW THEOLOGIANS WE HAVE NO RECORD OF WHAT THEY LOOKED LIKE SO FOR SOME WE HAVE PUT AN IDENTIKIT TOGETHER.

JUSTIN MARTYR

In the context of the first centuries, the early church needed to find its place in the thought and culture of its day. The **apologists** tried to make theology clear to those around them, and were often faced with persecution and harsh accusations.

Justin Martyr (c.100-c.165) was originally a philosopher, and perhaps one of the most important apologists. As a philosopher he came to see that true philosophy was actually found in the Christian gospel about Jesus. Aiming mainly at Jewish people, he concentrated on understanding who Jesus Christ was and what sort of relationship Jesus had with God.

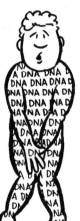

Justin used the idea of the

LOGOS

(the **Word**).

In Greek philosophy this was understood to be a principle behind the universe which brought unity, order and rationality to all things - similar in a way to how **DNA** brings shape and order to all living creatures.

16

The idea has roots in the Old Testament where God's word is involved in **creation** and **revelation**. For Justin, **Christ** himself was the **logos**, inspiring Greek philosophers before Jesus walked the earth, and being present in all human beings through the **Logos spermatikos** (the seed-bearing word, the spark or seed present in everyone).

The logos revealed itself in some ancient philosophy, in visions of the Old Testament, and eventually in the historical person of Jesus. So, in this way the opening verses of **John's gospel** could be interpreted as God's logos incarnate in Jesus (see John 1.1-14).

IN MUCH THE SAME WAY AS EVERYONE HAD DNA EVEN BEFORE SCIENTISTS DISCOVERED IT, SO JUSTIN THOUGHT THAT EVERYONE HAD THE SEED OF THE WORD AND KNEW SOMETHING OF IT, BUT THEY COULD ONLY KNOW IT FULLY WHEN IT CAME TO EARTH AS A HUMAN PERSON.

Justin used the image of sunlight to explain the relationship between Jesus and God. Jesus, the **Son**, is related to God, the **Father**, as the rays of light are to the sun. In later theology, this was to become inaccurate, as it depicts the Son as being subordinate and secondary to the Father.

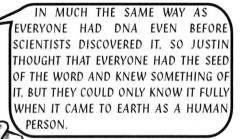

Agricola completes Roman invasion of Britain	Hadrian becomes Roman Emperor	Hadrian's Wall completed	Caladonians force Romans to retreat behind Hadrian's Wall
84	117	126	180

Ideas about **creation** were also explored by Justin. Most philosophy followed the idea that the universe was eternal. However, Justin believed that there was a beginning act of creation. Although not yet using the idea that the world was created **ex nihilo**, out of nothing, Justin contributed to this distinctive and Christian understanding about the origin of life.

 Justin's importance was that he attempted to integrate Christian faith with the prevailing philosophies of his time. Christianity arose as one idea among many, and therefore needed people to illustrate the sense and reason of such a faith. Justin ultimately died for this faith, hence his title of **martyr**.

IRENAEUS OF LYONS

Gnosticism is a general term for a variety of beliefs and movements which stressed the importance of knowledge (Greek **'gnosis'**) for salvation. In the early church it was widespread, and at times it appeared similar to early versions of Christianity.

Irenaeus (c.130-200) was **bishop of Lyons** in c.178, and became a leading defender of Christianity against the challenges of Gnosticism.

His major work... **Against Heresies** attempted to clearly mark out true Christian teaching on **matters of salvation** and the use of **tradition**.

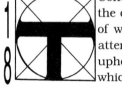 Concerning **Scripture**, Irenaeus insisted that the church's role in the **canon** (the fixed group of writings included in the **Bible**) was not an attempt to create Scripture, but to preserve and uphold it. Therefore, Scripture is something which does not change and has authority.

18

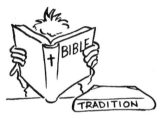

In order to interpret the Bible, Christians must do so in line with the **tradition of the church** running back to the earliest apostles.

This was contrary to some Gnostic claims which said they had some **secret inspiration** as to how to read the Bible.

For Irenaeus, there was a traditional way of interpreting the **tradition of Scripture!**

One Gnostic belief was that **matter itself was evil**. Irenaeus pointed out that if this were so, why was Christianity so affirmative of things like **bread** and **wine** in worship? In actual fact, the Son of Man affirmed creation by becoming human himself. In tracing human steps, experiencing this life that we all experience, Jesus brought back human life to perfection - he **'recapitulated'** human life.

> HE BECAME WHAT WE ARE IN ORDER TO ENABLE US TO BECOME WHAT HE IS.

This has implications for anthropology, the doctrine of humanity. Rather than being static or stuck in a rut, humans have the capacity for growth and maturity, given the correct circumstances.

Emperor Commodus assumes the title 'Britannicus' (British)	Christianity spreads to tribes north of Hadrian's Wall	St. Alban martyred for his faith
184	205	208

19

Irenaeus is key for his interaction with Gnosticism. One other important refutation involved the **Marcionite heresy**.

Named after **Marcion**, a prominent Gnostic, it taught that the God of the Old Testament and the God of the New Testament were **two separate Gods**.

OLD TESTAMENT | NEW TESTAMENT

SON FATHER HOLY SPIRIT

Irenaeus insisted that the same God operates throughout history and throughout the Bible. In the Bible, we see God's plan of salvation revealed in the work of the **Father**, the **Son**, and the **Holy Spirit**.

Using the term **'the economy of salvation'**, he attempted to explain God's role in this plan of salvation, and hence ground the **doctrine of God** in the experiences of Biblical life.

THE ROLE OF TRADITION

Throughout the Patristic period, and indeed the rest of Christian theology, **the role of tradition** has been extremely important. **Irenaeus** was fighting against those who thought they could interpret the Bible anyway they liked, without any thought for what other people had taught. **Tradition** was never seen by the fathers as an additional source to the Scriptures, but it preserved the teaching of the church to guard against heresy. This was to be important in the debates with **Arius** and others, and eventually **creeds** and **confessions** came to embody this tradition in order to help theology define itself in ages to come.

TRINITY AND CHRISTOLOGY

A large part of Patristic theology was concerned with two particular areas - the **doctrine of God**, and the **doctrine of Christ**.

THE DEBATES THAT TOOK PLACE CAN SEEM ODD AND POINTLESS, ESPECIALLY WHEN SO MUCH APPEARS TO HANG ON ONE PARTICULAR WORD, OR EVEN LETTER. NEVERTHELESS, THESE DEBATES ARE AT THE VERY HEART OF THEOLOGY, FOR THEIR ULTIMATE CONCERN IS WITH THE NATURE OF GOD.

Looking at the **New Testament** accounts of Jesus, early Christians saw a human being who soon came to be worshipped. People called Jesus **'Lord'**, and talked about things he said and did, which only God was supposed to say and do.

The question is, what do we make of Jesus? Was he a mere man, or some divine being? How can a mortal human be perfect and all powerful? How can a divine being suffer death on a cross.

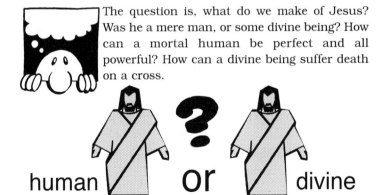

human **or** divine

Julius and Aaron put to death for their faith at Caerwent	Marcus Postumus creates a breakaway empire which includes Britain and Gaul	The Empire is restored
c259	260	274

Patristic theology soon marked out the boundaries.

Bring in the Holy Spirit, and you start talking in threes. Three Gods? **No**. Three modes? **No**. The boundaries were set at three persons (**Father**, **Son** and **Holy Spirit**) in one God. That's the easy part. The hardest part is to try and work out what that means. And that's where many theologians have appealed to **'mystery'**!

ORIGEN

As theology progressed and the Christian church grew, it was soon to split into the two different streams of **Eastern** and **Western** Christianity.

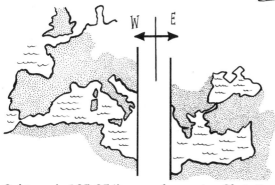

Origen became influential primarily in **Eastern** thought.

Origen (c.185-254) was born to Christian parents in **Alexandria**, and became a powerful influence in many circles, especially due to his teaching role in **Caesarea**. Devoting himself to reading the Bible, he came to develop important thinking regarding Scripture.

Mausaeus Carausius appointed to protect Britain from Frankish and Saxon pirates

Diocletian declares an empire-wide persecution of Christians

Nevertheless, Origen was condemned later in Christian history for his belief that the souls of human beings were **pre-existent** (rather than the idea that souls are created at a particular time by God), and believing in the doctrine of **apokatastasis** - that every creature would eventually be saved by God.

Origen was concerned with the proper way to read the **Bible**. Anyone who reads either Testament soon comes across difficult passages which are hard to understand. There are also ideas and stories that appear to have little relevance to everyday life.

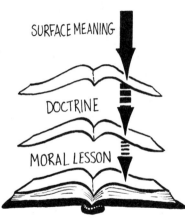

Origen distinguished between different meanings of Scripture - **a surface meaning**, and an **allegorical interpretation**. **The Holy Spirit**, who interprets the text for the person, allows the reader (depending on their enlightenment) to understand the **spiritual meaning** behind the text. This spiritual meaning could sometimes provide **doctrine**, and sometimes a **moral lesson**, therefore giving a possible threefold understanding to each text.

In Christology Origen developed a theology which saw a distinction between the **Father** and the **Son**. Both were of the same nature, but the Father had priority over the Son because the Son is eternally generated by the Father.

Constantine declared co-emperor by troops in Britain **Flavius Severus and Constantine agree on more tolerance for Christians**

He illustrated this in the following way:

> IF A LUMP OF IRON IS CONSTANTLY KEPT IN A FIRE, IT WILL ABSORB ITS HEAT THROUGH ALL ITS PORES AND VEINS. IF THE FIRE IS CONTINUOUS, AND THE IRON IS NOT REMOVED, IT BECOMES TOTALLY CONVERTED TO THE OTHER ... IN THE SAME WAY, THE SOUL WHICH HAS BEEN CONSTANTLY PLACED IN THE LOGOS AND WISDOM OF GOD, IS GOD IN ALL THAT IT DOES, FEELS, AND UNDERSTANDS.

It may be that later this thought influenced the theology of **Arius**.

Origen is one theologian with many facets. His scheme of the world, where eternal spirits choose evil, become human and are then redeemed by Christ in this world (or perhaps others) is complete and attractive. He also refuted attacks of philosophers of the time in, for example, his book **Contra Celsum**...

Against Celsus

Nevertheless, his main legacy for the orthodox church was to be his understanding of how to read the Bible.

The Battle of Milvian Bridge. Constantine wins after seeing a vision of a Christian symbol

Constantine becomes absolute ruler of the Western Empire

TERTULLIAN

Tertullian (c.160-225) trained as a lawyer and was only converted to Christianity halfway through his life. He was a priest in **Carthage**, and his main impact was on the **Western** church, becoming the first great Latin father.

His most notable work has to do with the **doctrine of the Trinity**. He was the first to use the term, **'trinity'**, and he attempted to clarify what was meant by a **'person'** in this context. He defined a person as someone who performs actions and says words.

THE LATIN **PERSONA** MEANS A **MASK**, AND WAS USED TO DESCRIBE MASKS IN THE THEATRE WHICH ACTORS WORE TO TAKE ON DIFFERENT PARTS.

However, when God was described as **one substance** and **three persons**, Tertullian would not have meant that there were three Gods, but rather a single God acting through three persons throughout history - **Father**, **Son** and **Spirit**.

This is known as an **economic Trinity**.

Yet how can we understand the relationships of these three persons? Tertullian described them as **distinct** (yet not divided), and **different** (yet not separate).

Constantine publicly converts to Christianity

Christianity becomes the official religion of the Roman Empire

Such a definition was against the **Monarchians** who saw no distinctions in a Godhead which only assumed the different roles at different times in history. Tertullian proceeded along his route as he thought that this was faithful to the Bible.

Concerning Scripture, Tertullian opposed the Gnostic heresies of **Marcion**. The whole Bible was the authority for the church, able to lead into the knowledge of God and salvation. However, he also insisted on the role of the tradition of the church (**the rule of faith**) which was required to prevent the false interpretations given by heretics.

Tertullian later became involved with a group called the **Montanists** who concentrated on prophetic visions and charismatic experiences. Due to their extremes, Montanists were later condemned by the church, yet Tertullian's influence lived on, especially in debates concerning **Christology** and the **Trinity**.

Council of Arles called by Constantine

Constantine declares Sunday to be a day of rest

ARIUS, ARIANISM +NICAEA

A notorious figure in the early church **Arius (c.250-336** and his followers forced one of the greatest debates of the early church, and the formation of a council to try and resolve it.

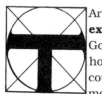

Arius was a priest in **Alexandria** who was **excommunicated** for his views. He believed in God's **uniqueness**, and therefore could not hold that God could be more than one. This meant that the Son, although a special creature who was created first, and although perfect, **was not the same as God**.

GOD

JESUS

The controversy grew, and **Constantine I**, emperor of Rome, called a council at **Nicaea** in 325. The first of the great ecumenical councils (bringing all of Christendom together) produced a creed to combat **Arianism**. The council affirmed that the Son was of the **same substance** with the Father, for the Son was **begotten** of the Father - that is, not made out of nothing, but out of the Father. The important phrase is **homoousios**, which proclaims that the Son **'is of one substance with the Father'**. Although not a Scriptural word, it made it clear that Arius' views were excluded.

one substance

FATHER

SON

2
8

NEVERTHELESS, THE COUNCIL DID NOT HAVE THE EFFECT DESIRED, AS ARIANISM ONLY WENT QUIET AND THEN REAPPEARED LATER. THE REAL EFFECT WAS TO SPLIT THE CHURCH INTO TWO. THERE WERE THOSE WHO, ANTI-ARIUS, AFFIRMED **THE ONENESS OF GOD** (WHILST NOT DENYING THE THREE PERSONS). AND THOSE WHO, REALLY FOLLOWING ORIGEN AND NOT ARIUS, AFFIRMED **THE THREENESS OF GOD** (WHILST NOT DENYING THE ONENESS).

GOD

SON   FATHER   HOLY SPIRIT

As one of the most important debates in theology, it can often appear irrelevant. Yet the vital questions remain - how can God be both one and three, and how can Jesus be both God and man? The answers to these questions would be fundamental for the rest of theology.

Emperor Thodosius outlaws all forms of pagen worship	St. Ninian begins conversion of the Picts in Scotland	St. Patrick sold into slavery to Ireland
391	397	401

ATHANASIUS

Into all this ferment of doctrine, many different churchmen were to make their contribution. Many were vital, but perhaps none more so than **Athanasius**.

Educated in **Alexandria**, **Athanasius** (c.297-373) was the aide to a bishop who visited the **Council of Nicaea**. From there he retained a strong stance against Arianism, and became bishop of **Alexandria** from 328 until his death.

The key to Athanasius' theology and his vital role in Christian history is what he had to say about the **doctrine of Christ**. **De incarnatione**...

On The Incarnation

was written as a defence of the idea that Jesus was actually **God in human nature**.

His argument was with the **Arians** who believed that Christ was not completely God, and also with some **Origenists**.

Athanasius taught that if Christ were not God, then **Jesus as a saviour** was an impossible idea. How can one creature save another? The essence of what it is to be a creature is the necessity to be saved.

SAVE ME!

If Jesus is just like any other creature, then salvation through Christ is not possible. If Arius was correct in his Christology, then the church was guilty of **idolatry**, that is worshipping something other than God. The church must look to God and what he has done, not to what we think and reason.

FOR HE BECAME HUMAN THAT WE MIGHT BECOME DIVINE.

Although exiled several times after **Nicaea** when Arianism gained some influence, Athanasius' contribution was enormous.

AS WELL AS ATTACKING ARIANISM, HE HELPED BRING RECONCILIATION BETWEEN THE **ANTIOCHENES** (THOSE IN THE WEST WITH HIM WHO STRESSED ONENESS IN GOD) AND THOSE IN THE EAST WHO EMPHASISED THREENESS, AFTER **ORIGEN**.

Such a reconciliation is seen in the **Cappadocian Fathers** and the **Council of Constantinople**.

GOD

SON / FATHER HOLY SPIRIT

Athanasius was also famous for his recognition of the 27 books of the **New Testament** as being **canonical**, which he referred to in a letter of 367. However, his enduring influence must be on the doctrine of Christ, and so the doctrine of God.

New Testament

One of the contemporary questions which Muslims put to Christians is how can God be three and one at the same time. What would Athanasius' answer have been?

THE CAPPADOCIAN FATHERS

The business of **Christology** and then defining the **Trinity** continued. Three figures from **Cappadocia** came into this debate -

Basil of Caesarea,   **Gregory of Nazianzus**,   and his brother **Gregory of Nyssa**

HOWDY!   HI!   NICE TO MEET YOU.

Each of the three figures had their own roles to play, but they are chiefly remembered for their **opposition to Arianism** and the role they played in defining the Trinity. Following on from what had gone before, they searched to give some meaning to the idea of God being one substance (**homoousios**) in three beings (**hypostases**).

To understand this we need to understand the idea of
universals and **particulars.**

There is a universal idea of **dogs**. But within that universal, there are particular instances of what it is to be a dog, say a **terrier** or a **poodle**.

The same is true of many things - chairs, tables, and also human beings. In the same way, the **one substance** is the universal **'God'**, and the **three hypostases** are particular instances of what it is to be God, namely **Father**, **Son** and **Holy Spirit**.

dogs

TERRIER   POODLE

GOD

SON   FATHER   HOLY SPIRIT

So, their understanding of the Trinity developed in the face of the **Arians** and the **Macedonians** (who denied the divinity of the Holy Spirit). But the **Cappadocians** faced the charge that they actually believed in three Gods (**tritheism**), as their analogy with universals and particulars fell down at this point.

The Cappadocians brought many strands of early Christian thought together. In addition, they refuted many heresies. This included the **Apollinarian** threat which believed that Jesus did not have a human soul, to which they replied that Jesus had to be fully human in order to save completely.

CONSTANTINOPLE

But their main contribution was to **Trinitarian doctrine**. At the council of **Constantinople** in 381 the two **Gregorys** took an active part in a meeting which affirmed the decrees of **Nicaea** and included the **Holy Spirit** in the formulation.

AMBROSE

Another foe of Arianism, **Ambrose** (339-397)' was born into a noble Roman family and became a governor before he was ordained bishop of **Milan** in 374. He attacked Arianism both theologically and politically, and reflected on the nature of the relationship between the church and the state. He believed that the elements (bread and wine) in the Lord's supper changed in nature during the sacrament, and this was to pave the way for the doctrine of **transubstantiation**. He is also known for having instructed and baptised **Augustine**.

St. Patrick begins conversion of the Irish	Last Roman legion leaves Britain	Rome sacked by Visigoths
405	406	410

AUGUSTINE

Arguably the most famous and influential of the Christian fathers, **Aurelius Augustine** (354-430) hardly left any area of Christian theology untouched. At the age of 32 he believed that he was miraculously guided by God to pick up and read Paul's letter to the Romans, and through the reading of this he was converted. Much of his energy was directed in writing against **Manicheism**, a widely influential Gnostic group of the time, and so combating various beliefs such as **determinism**, **dualism** and their view of Scripture. In 395 he became bishop of **Hippo**, and there became engaged in fierce theological debate.

His great work, **De civitate Dei**.... drew a picture of two cities, that of the world and that of God, and the contrasts between them.

The City of God

The end result is a presentation of the whole Christian faith in a systematic fashion, as never had been achieved before.

The theological battles he fought occurred on many fronts. The issue of **grace** and **free will** concerned him in the **Pelagian** controversy.

4

Taking its name from a British monk, **Pelagius**, Pelagianism argued for the need for moral achievement and improvement within the ranks of the Christian church. This gave the appearance that there was no place for grace, God's unconditional love and mercy, in the plan of salvation.

In opposition to this, Augustine insisted that grace was vital to Christian life, in its beginning, continuation, and end. In fact, men and women are so utterly corrupt that without God they could not even respond to the gospel.

Why are human beings unable to reach God? Augustine's doctrine of the **fall** meant that all men and women are biased against God, being contaminated by **original sin**. This refers not just to the first sin of Adam and Eve, but to the fact that all are evil by nature because all took part in that **first sin**.

So where does this leave Pelagius? According to Augustine, without hope - for only by God's initiative can this debilitating situation be reversed.

In actual fact, Pelagius thought that human beings do have the capacity to reform and **save themselves**, where salvation is a reward for **good works**. Such a central and thorny issue was resolved by the **Council of Carthage** (418), which condemned the views of Pelagius. However, this was not the last to be heard of such views ...

CARTHAGE

Emperor Honorius writes to the Britons telling them they must now defend themselves

Attila the Hun attacks Western Europe

3
5

410   445

Church and sacraments were debated with the **Donatists**. They argued that the church was an exclusive place for the saved, in which there was no room for sinners.

During the persecution by the **Emperor Diocletian**, some Christians surrendered their Scriptures and so were accused by the Donatists of betraying the church. They argued that these **traditores** should therefore be excluded.

Augustine argued that the church was a mix of both saints and sinners, only to be perfected at the end of time. We cannot separate them as humans, but this did not matter, for it was not the holiness of the ministers which was necessary for a holy church, but rather the holiness of Christ.

So, when a priest offered the sacrament of mass (**the Lord's Supper**), it is Christ's sacrifice on the cross which is important, not what the priest has or has not done. Such views had important consequences for **ecclesiology** (the doctrine of the church).

Finally, Augustine contributed to the **doctrine of the Trinity**. He included the **Spirit** in the **Godhead**, and refused any notion of **subordination**. Yet how did the Trinity work? Augustine used several models to help understand this. In the human sphere we see a trio of **mind**, **knowledge** and **love** as active in our rational processes. **Memory**, **understanding** and **will** parallel this trio. Such trios are images of what God is in himself like, three **'parts'** relating to one **'whole'**.

human

MIND   LOVE

KNOWLEDGE

An important point in his doctrine of the Trinity is the affirmation of the **origin of the Spirit**. This matter is central to the debate known as the **filioque** ('and from the Son') controversy. Did the Spirit proceed from the Father alone, or from both the Father and the Son?

The Greek theologians maintained the distinction, arguing that the **Spirit proceeds from the Father**, whilst the Son is begotten of the Father. Therefore God the Father is the sole source of being, there are not two distinct sources.

However, Augustine argued that, because in the New Testament Jesus gives the Spirit to his disciples, so the **Spirit proceeds from both Father and Son**.

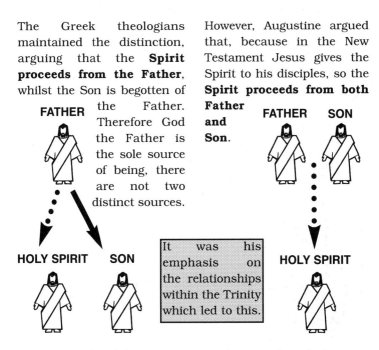

FATHER

HOLY SPIRIT   SON

FATHER   SON

HOLY SPIRIT

It was his emphasis on the relationships within the Trinity which led to this.

In the end, this debate was to contribute to the split between the **Eastern** and **Western** churches (c.1054) and is still a contended issue.

To read Christian theology without looking at Augustine would be a mistake. Love him or hate him, he has become the **father** of all succeeding **orthodox theology**, both Catholic and Protestant.

Jutes, Angles, and Saxons begin invasions of Britain	Last Roman Emperor deposed	Battle of Badon: British victory over the Saxons (led by King Arthur?)
449	476	c500

COUNCIL OF EPHESUS

431

As theology developed, so more questions arose.

If Jesus was God and man, what role did they leave for **Mary**?

Was she the mother of the human Jesus but not of the divine Jesus?

In the 5th century, **Nestorius** claimed that Mary could only be called the bearer of Christ's humanity, thus emphasising the separateness of the human and divine natures.

human

divine

This had the effect of denying any real union between the human and the divine. **Cyril of Alexandria** opposed this view, and under **Emperor Theodosius II** the **Council of Ephesus** was called. There the term **'theotokos'** was approved, stating that Mary was the bearer of God the Son. This therefore emphasised the unity of Christ's person, both God and human.

COUNCIL OF CHALCEDON

451

Yet another council was called in **Chalcedon**, a council that was to give the most important statement about Christ yet. The council was brought together by **Pope Leo I** (pope 440-461) who fought against the Christology of **Eutyches**. This proposed a form of **monophysitism** (the doctrine that Christ has only one nature - that nature is divine). However, Eutyches mixed the two natures together and so blurred the divine and the human. Before the council Leo had written his **Tome** to **Bishop Flavian** in **Constantinople** as a refutation of these views. Leo thought that Eutyches was claiming that in Christ there was

JESUS

human divine

no real human flesh descended from Mary. The council then built on Leo's work, defining that Jesus Christ was one divine person in two natures, one human, one divine. Christ is **homoousios** with the Father and with human nature, and **"made known in two natures without confusion, without change, without division, without separation."**

BOETHIUS

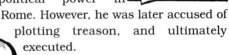

Born to Roman parents, **Boethius** (c.480-524) was a thinker who achieved significant political power in Rome. However, he was later accused of plotting treason, and ultimately executed.

THINK ON THIS ONE BOETHIUS!

39

At a time when most education went through the control of the church, Boethius was one of the few who kept up an interest in the world of **philosophy**.

 Boethius' main task was to bring **Christianity** together with **Greek philosophy** from the likes of **Aristotle** and the **Neoplatonists**. Whether he should be included in the 'patristic period' or the 'medieval period' is open to question,

FOR HE ACTS AS A BRIDGE BETWEEN THE TWO ERAS.

PATRISTIC

MEDIEVAL

It was largely only through his work that the tradition of philosophy was kept alive, until the likes of **Anselm** and **Aquinas** opened it up again.

St Columba lands at Iona to Christianise the people of Scotland	**St Asaph in Wales**	**Augustine becomes the first archbishop of Canterbury**
563	570	598

Boethius believed that the **'highest good'**, a concept used by philosophers, was the same as the **Christian God**. During his imprisonment he wrote...

The Consolation of Philosophy

c523

exploring both the nature of **philosophy** and the **concept of God**. The work has been criticised for depending too much on philosophy, and ignoring the role of faith and the Scriptures. Boethius seemed to trust his **philosophy** more than his **faith**, and although a Christian, **neoplatonic** philosophy appeared to be more important for him.

Boethius opens up the debate about the relationship between philosophy and faith. What is the role of philosophy, can the two be integrated, and which is the more important? Can you do theology without philosophy, or are the two opposed?

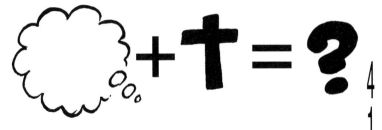

MAXIMUS THE CONFESSOR

For many theologians in the West, it is easy to ignore the **Eastern theologians** who continued in their own tradition.

Eastern theology continued to be concerned with **Christology**, and at the time of **Maximus** (c.580-662) it insisted that there was only one will in Christ in order to please the **monophysite** party.

JESUS

human   divine

Maximus, an aristocrat who became a monk, opposed this. He defended the idea that within Christ there were two wills, one **divine**, one **human**.

During his life he had to flee **Byzantium**, but was eventually forced to return and punished for his refusal to recant his views.

Maximus was also influential in the development of **mystical theology**, where the goal of a Christian life is the mystical vision of God.

46

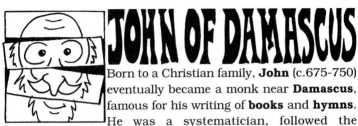

JOHN OF DAMASCUS

Born to a Christian family, **John** (c.675-750) eventually became a monk near **Damascus**, famous for his writing of **books** and **hymns**. He was a systematician, followed the **Trinitarian** theology of the **Cappadocian fathers**, and affirmed the unity of Christ in **two natures**. He promoted **asceticism**, the withdrawal of the church from the world and its trappings, and defended the use of **icons** and **images** in worship, against the attacks of the **iconoclasts**. Such issues relate to the theology of creation and redemption.

The issue of **icons** fuelled a controversy which was to be resolved at the second council of **Nicaea** (787), where it

787

NICAEA II

was stated that it is acceptable to portray Christ in the form of images because of what has happened in the **incarnation**, where Christ came as a creature. This decision was ultimately rejected by the **Protestants** during the **Reformation**, but was accepted by the **Roman church** and became increasingly important for the **Eastern church**.

47

There were many other disputes in early theology, many other great theologians, and many fine examples of Christian scholarship. All of these influenced the church to a great extent.

A brief overview is all we can have, but towards the end of this period, during the 8th century, appeared...

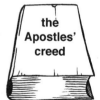

the Apostles' creed

INCLUDED IN IT ARE STATEMENTS FROM AS EARLY AS THE 2ND CENTURY, BUT IT ACTS AS A SUMMARY OF CHRISTIAN BELIEF AND IS A PRODUCT OF THE MANY COUNCILS, DEBATES AND CREEDS WE HAVE SEEN.

It is a link between the patristic period and the rest of Christian history, for it embodies the theology of that age which even today affects the worship and lives of millions of Christians.

THE

PERIOD

Sometimes called the **Middle Ages**, this period of history between the end of the **Roman empire** and the beginning of the **Renaissance** is often seen as a period in Christian history where thought and practice went into decline.

> WHILST AT THE BEGINNING OF THE PERIOD IT MAY HAVE SEEMED THAT WAY, THEOLOGIANS CONTINUED TO REFLECT ON THE WORLD AND GOD, USUALLY WITHIN THE CONTEXT OF A RELIGIOUS COMMUNITY.

Around the **thirteenth century** much new and radical thought was required in the light of philosophies which were rediscovered, particularly the work of **Aristotle**. Although towards the end of the middle ages the church appeared to decline, the medieval period should never be forgotten as a vital part of theology. Time and again, theology seeks to understand faith and place it in the context of the day, and this is as true for the 'middle ages' as it was for the patristic period, and is for today.

ANSELM

During the tenth and eleventh centuries a movement known as **scholasticism** began. Education was moved out of the church into institutions of learning, and the growing influence of philosophy needed to be understood and brought together with Christian theology.

Logic, reason, understanding - all of these and more were characteristics of this movement which tried to understand the faith better.

Anselm (c.1033-1109) was born in Italy, but travelled to Normandy to become a monk, and then eventually he went to Canterbury in 1093 to be archbishop. He is often considered to be one of the founders of scholasticism, and brought theology and philosophy together.

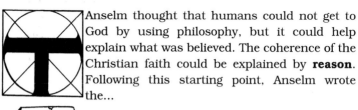

Anselm thought that humans could not get to God by using philosophy, but it could help explain what was believed. The coherence of the Christian faith could be explained by **reason**. Following this starting point, Anselm wrote the...

Monologion

which provided a 'proof' of God's existence. This argued that because we can see different types of 'good', there must be an ultimate 'good'. To be ultimately good, it must also be ultimately great, the greatest of all beings, that is, God.

Vikings control England

1013

4
6

This argument works by believing that universals (concepts such as 'dog', 'human', 'table', and 'chair') are in fact more real than particular examples and instances of them (for example, poodles or terriers, in the case of the universal 'dog').

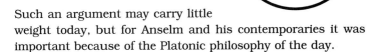

Such an argument may carry little weight today, but for Anselm and his contemporaries it was important because of the Platonic philosophy of the day.

Later in the...

Proslogion

Anselm provided a classic argument for the existence of God, known as the **ontological argument**. This defined God as 'that, than which nothing greater can be conceived'. God must exist in order to be the greatest being. If he did not exist, he would not be that greatest being.

IF GOD DOESN'T EXIST, WE COULD IMAGINE SOMETHING GREATER, NAMELY A GOD THAT DOES EXIST. SINCE WE CAN CONCEIVE OF THIS GREATER GOD, GOD HIMSELF MUST EXIST FOR OTHERWISE AN EVEN GREATER ONE WOULD. SO GOD EXISTS.

Confusing? A fellow monk, **Gaunilo,** challenged Anselm with a work **On Behalf of the Fool**, because Anselm had been convinced that the ontological argument was strong enough to make even the fool believe!

Apart from such reasoning, Anselm is also remembered for...

Cur Deus Homo

('Why God Became Man'). This is an exploration of the incarnation and of the cross (which Anselm believed by revelation and faith, not because of argument). Because of sin, human beings had failed to give due honour to God. A **satisfaction** of this honour is needed by either punishing humans, or by offering something to God to provide this satisfaction.

Humans could not be punished in this way, but the satisfaction could only be paid by God. What could God do? The answer is that he became human, a God-man, so that humanity offered the satisfaction, but God paid it. Such a satisfaction took place on the cross, and so the death of Christ, the God-man, was necessary.

SATISFACTION PAID

Anselm's legacy in the areas of philosophy and theology are great. His understanding of atonement was to have a huge impact on the Christian world, and even though he may have pushed reason further than some may have liked, his arguments were to be taken up by many philosophers and theologians in later times.

In *Cur Deus Homo?* Anselm used the idea of **honour**.

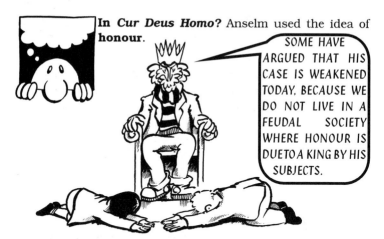

SOME HAVE ARGUED THAT HIS CASE IS WEAKENED TODAY, BECAUSE WE DO NOT LIVE IN A FEUDAL SOCIETY WHERE HONOUR IS DUE TO A KING BY HIS SUBJECTS.

Is this fair, and how much is our thinking about theology determined by our context (the society, culture and world in which we live)?

Macbeth becomes King of Scotland	Harold becomes the last Saxon King of England	William the Conqueror invades England	Tower of London begins to be built
1057	1066		1078

PETER ABELARD

Peter Abelard (1079-c.1142) was born in Brittany, and educated by two noted philosophers, **Roscelin** and **William of Champeaux**. He became famous not just for his theology, but for his love affair with **Heloise**, which ended with tragedy and humiliation.

Abelard's two mentors taught opposing ideas about **universals**.

dogs

Roscelin was a **nominalist** (believing that universals were just a convention or a name).

William was a **realist** (believing that the class actually refers to something real).

One of Abelard's achievements was to mediate between these two positions, saying that the universal idea is a concept in our mind. However, this concept existed before the creation of anything in that class and in this way Abelard found a middle path. Such a position was to remain common for several centuries.

Domesday Book is completed	The First Crusade begins	Jerusalem captured by the Crusaders	First court held at Westminster
1086	1096	1099	

49

 Abelard wrote **Sic et Non** ('Yes and No'), which used the **dialectical** method of reasoning, whereby truth is reached by weighing all the issues together. Truth is not attained by simply quoting tradition (although tradition is vitally important), but by the use of reason as well. Doubting and asking questions was important to Abelard, so that reason could therefore be used to show Christians what to believe (not, as with Anselm, using reason to understand what Christians already believe).

Atonement was something which Abelard approached in this way....

ONE PREVAILING UNDERSTANDING HAD BEEN THAT CHRIST HAD DIED IN ORDER TO PAY THE RANSOM WHICH GOD OWED TO THE DEVIL (WHO HELD HUMANKIND CAPTIVE).

But Abelard rejected this idea, together with the idea that the ransom was paid to God himself.

Rather, Christ died as an extreme example of God's love for humanity. This is known as the **'moral influence theory'** of the atonement.

EXAMPLE OF GOD'S LOVE

 Abelard took steps towards a more modern way of thinking, whereby reason takes on a greater role.

Henry I becomes King of England

1100

His thought on the cross has also been of great importance, taken on board to a great extent by modern **liberal Protestantism**.

 Does Abelard's theory of the atonement make sense of all that Scripture says about Christ's death? It may be part of the story, but if there was no other explanation, would Christ's death actually show God's love, or would it rather be an act of ultimate failure?

PETER LOMBARD

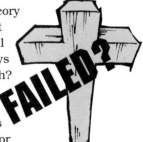

Peter Lombard (c.1100-60) taught in Paris and became a bishop in 1159. He is remembered for his..

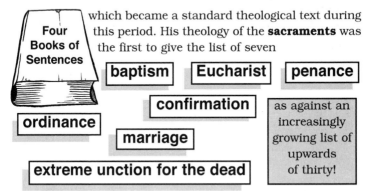

Four Books of Sentences which became a standard theological text during this period. His theology of the **sacraments** was the first to give the list of seven

baptism **Eucharist** **penance**

confirmation

ordinance as against an increasingly growing list of upwards of thirty!

marriage

extreme unction for the dead

Instead of defining a sacrament as only an outward sign of an inward grace, Lombard also maintained that the act itself was the **effective cause** of that grace. That is, there was something special happening at the time of the sacrament, something caused by that act. Such thinking was to remain the prevailing view in the Roman Catholic Church, but one which the Protestant Reformers were to contest.

FRANCIS OF ASSISI

Within this period of the church, Christian life, thought and action centred on religious communities. These were places where people who were devoted to the faith (usually men) lived their whole lives, learning about theology and philosophy, and reflecting on the world in the midst of a deeply religious grouping.

Francis (1182-1226) was brought up in the midst of luxury and he dreamt of fame.

Eventually he founded a religious order (1210) which became known as the **Franciscans**.

However, in his early years he had a dramatic religious conversion. The result was that he roamed the countryside dressed only in a cloak, teaching a growing group of followers.

Francis' aim was to imitate the life of Christ. This was achieved through devout humility, poverty and simplicity. He is remembered for his love of nature. He is said to have preached a sermon to the birds, saying...

MY BROTHER BIRDS, MUCH OUGHT YOU TO PRAISE YOUR CREATOR AND LOVE HIM...

In addition, he gave respect to women in a society which often put women on a much lower ranking than men.

Francis was obedient to the pope, and so a radical group of Christian people who lived their lives amongst the rest of the world was accepted into the mainstream church.

Francis claimed to receive the **'stigmata'** after meditating on the sufferings of Christ. These are the wounds that Christ received on the cross, and are said to have appeared on Francis' body. This tradition was to be followed in later Christian lives of deep meditation and spirituality.

The Franciscans were to become an important order throughout the thirteenth century.

Francis helped many to live a radical lifestyle, to reject all property and become completely poor. The aim was to become more Christ like, and although the devotion of Francis is not in doubt, soon the Franciscans made exceptions to their rules of poverty and became extremely wealthy in time.

THEOLOGY, HOWEVER, SHOULD ADDRESS THE QUESTIONS OF WEALTH AND PERSONAL DEVOTION AS MUCH AS ANY OTHER THEOLOGICAL QUESTIONS, AND FRANCIS IS A TIMELY REMINDER OF THIS.

After Henry's death Stephen claims throne and becomes King

1135

The start of the civil war between Stephen and Matilda

1138

Oxford University established

1163

THOMAS AQUINAS

Scholasticism had been growing, rediscovering Aristotle, and attempting to remain true to Christ and the traditions of the church. Whilst some rejected Aristotle and his philosophy, others adopted it wholesale. What was needed was someone to combine the two.

HELP!

Thomas Aquinas (1225-1274) was a Dominican monk (even though his mother opposed this and kept him in a castle for a year!) who taught in Paris and Italy. He adopted Aristotle's thinking, but instead of uncritically using it, he put it in a Christian form by accepting some parts, and rejecting others.

Aquinas wrote huge amounts of material and discussed many questions. His greatest work was a systematic presentation of the Christian faith in the...

Summa Theologicae

On the question of faith and reason, he argued that faith is based in Scripture and so is revealed. However, arguments also exist which support this faith, and which show the probability of what is believed. We know about the incarnation through revelation. We know what rocks are made up of through experience and reason. However, some things, such as the existence of God, can be known by both revelation and reason.

Aquinas provided **five** ways which could be used to show that God exists. These included the following ideas:-

That because everything has a cause, there must be an ultimate first cause.

Because everything changes, there must be something that doesn't change which causes this change.

Because there are different levels of excellence, this implies that there is a perfect being, that is God.

In opposition to Aristotle, Aquinas affirmed that God had created the world ex nihilo, out of nothing, rather than believing that the world was eternal.

0+0=

Aquinas also looked at how we can talk about God, a God who is so completely different from our world and what we know. God is only known by **analogy**. That is, we may call God 'good', but only if we understand good in a completely different way from how we usually use it, and take away from our idea of 'good' any of the limited notions it has when we talk of a dog being good, or a human being good, for example.

Aquinas was later approved as a teacher and doctor of the church, with the Summa becoming a standard resource. He also taught much about ethics, arguing that human beings have a **natural law** within them which acts as a guide to how we live our lives. All in all, Aquinas was a great systematician, bringing many things together into a great system, interacting with the important thought of his day.

Cambridge University established	Genghis Khan captures Peking	John signs Magna Carta
1209	1214	1215

JOHN DUNS SCOTUS

To have an insult named after you may be something you might not wish to be famous for. But **Duns Scotus'** (c.1265-1309) name was formed into the word **'Dunce'** by those who later disagreed with him! A Scottish Franciscan who taught in Oxford, Cambridge and Paris, he is known for his difficult writing and style. He produced commentaries on **Lombard's** *Sentences* and works on various theological questions.

In opposition to **Thomas Aquinas** who emphasised that reason and knowledge held first place over the **will**, Scotus stressed that humans have a freedom to choose what they will. This was important for understanding how human beings know things, and how they act.

Applying this to God, Scotus argued that God is free to act as he wills. For example, Jesus died on the cross not because he had to (as Anselm had argued), but because God had freely chosen to. In fact, the Son would have become human and died on the cross even if humans had not originally sinned.

GOD'S FREE CHOICE

Scotus, although using philosophy to his benefit, believed that much more of the faith was due to revelation than perhaps Aquinas had allowed.

5 6 0	Kublai Khan becomes Governor of China	The House of Commons is established	William Wallace leads a revolt in Scotland	Robert the Bruce becomes King of Scotland
	1242	1265	1297	1306

Scotus is also noted as a theologian who argued that it was probable that Mary was born without sin, the idea of the **immaculate conception**. Because Christ is the perfect redeemer, he must have redeemed one person whilst on earth. For this Scotus is remembered as the **'Marian Doctor'**.

It is important to remember figures like Scotus because when we look at people such as Aquinas we may get the impression that all theology was the same and everyone agreed on everything. Scotus was a reaction to Aquinas and his followers (**Thomists**), yet he still maintained room for a healthy relationship between faith and reason.

WILLIAM OF OCKHAM

Following in the scholastic tradition, **William of Ockham** (c. 1285-1349) was a pupil of Scotus, studied at Oxford, and taught on the Bible and Lombard. He was, however, accused of heresy by the chancellor of the university, and had to go to Avignon to face charges where he was ultimately excommunicated.

Ockham is important for his views on **universals**, which reversed much contemporary wisdom. He was a **nominalist**, and believed that universals do not exist in themselves, they are only known through the generalisations of other individuals. Only these individuals exist. A consequence is that we are unable to use things that do not exist to argue towards other things. For example, we cannot therefore argue in this way that God exists.

Edward II murdered	The start of the Hundred Years' War between England and France
1327	1337

5
7

His consistent use of logic insisted that philosophers could not argue their way to particular ideas of God (for example, being one, or being omnipotent, or being immortal). Only divine revelation is able to provide these things.

YAKITY YAK

It is possible that Ockham's rejection of philosophy in this way led to the growth of Christian **mysticism**. Yet he was not opposed to the use of logic, only to the unnecessary twists and arguments of the scholastics. Because of this he is known for **'Ockham's razor'**, a principle which argues that the simplest form of a statement is superior to an endless and complicated argument.

IT IS VAIN TO DO WITH MORE WHAT CAN BE DONE WITH FEWER.

THOMAS Á KEMPIS

A German monk and writer, **Thomas a Kempis** (1379-1471) is thought to have written the...

Imitation of Christ

a well known devotional work of theology. Self-denial, humility, trust and acceptance of God's love were key themes, themes that reappear throughout Christian history. Thomas taught these principles in small communities which stressed the moral example which Christ was and is for humans.

58

JOHN WYCLIFFE

As the medieval period headed towards a close, resentment of the church grew due to the abuses of its power. Not many people spoke out, but the radical voice of **John Wycliffe** (c.1329-84) was one which could not be silenced easily. Born in Yorkshire, he was a priest and a student at Oxford where he remained as a teacher.

He stood in the scholastic tradition, and turned his mind to many issues. One of these was the relationship between church and state, developing a theology of **dominion**. This argued that humanity was God's steward of the world, but only political power could be given to those who are made righteous by God's grace. Any mortal sin would take away the right to this power. He was thought to be condemning the church of the time, and so was condemned himself by declarations from the pope in 1377.

GOD'S GRACE

MAN'S STEWARDSHIP

In his later life he began to oppose what he saw as difficulties within the church. He argued that Scripture was more authoritative than both the pope and the church. This caused him to implement a scheme to have the Latin Bible (the **'vulgate'**) translated into English, so that all people could read it and see the witness to Christ throughout it.

THE BIBLE

The Black Death reaches Britain	Robin Hood first appears in ballads	Geoffrey Chaucer starts the Canterbury Tales	Henry V beats the French at Agincourt	
1348	1375	1387	1415	

Wycliffe attacked the wealth of the church, the presumption of its bishops, and the necessity of having a priest at communion. In addition he criticised the doctrine of **transubstantiation** which said that the elements of bread and wine used in the sacrament changed their nature to become Christ's body and blood during the service. For Wycliffe the elements were not mere symbols (just representing something), but Christ's body and blood were really present in the same way that a person's soul was present. However, he rejected the usual idea of transubstantiation.

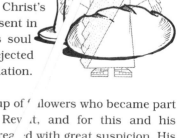

Wycliffe had a group of followers who became part of the Peasants' Revolt, and for this and his theology he was treated with great suspicion. His influence extended to an important continental theologian, **John Hus** in Prague, through his teaching of some Czech students who were at Oxford. Ultimately, Wycliffe was expelled from Oxford, and after his death his body was dug up and burnt due to his supposed heresies.

FOR ALL THIS WYCLIFFE IS OFTEN KNOWN AS THE MORNING STAR OF THE REFORMATION FOR THE WAY IN WHICH HE PREFIGURED THE COMING CHANGE.

THE MEDIEVAL PERIOD, OFTEN SEEN AS BARREN AND DARK,

WAS ACTUALLY A TIME OF GREAT THEOLOGICAL REFLECTION. PHILOSOPHY AND THEOLOGY WERE BROUGHT TOGETHER, AND CONSIDERATION WAS GIVEN TO ALL THE IMPORTANT THEMES OF CHRISTIAN THEOLOGY.

IT WAS TO PROVIDE THE BACKDROP FOR THE NEXT GREAT PERIOD, THE REFORMATION, WHICH WAS TO REAPPRAISE CHRISTIAN THEOLOGY IN MANY DRASTIC WAYS.

It may be noticed that the disputes of the Patristic period had to some extent gone. There were no long debates on

Christology   and the Trinity

(although they were discussed). As theology moves on, so does the world, and so the questions and issues change to meet the very real needs of the day.

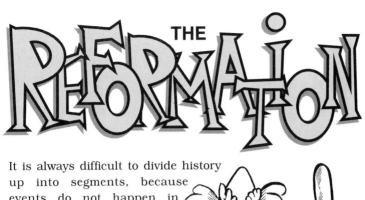

THE REFORMATION

It is always difficult to divide history up into segments, because events do not happen in isolation. However, from the beginning of the sixteenth century onwards a clear change in attitudes and thinking took place...

GENERALLY KNOWN AS THE REFORMATION.

Theological considerations were of great importance, as the following pages indicate. However, there were also other factors that promoted change, especially political considerations.

Above all, however, it is the theological debates and controversies of this period and beyond which was to change the shape of the church into the way we see it today.

DESIDERIUS ERASMUS

Erasmus is often described as the person who lay the egg for the **Reformation**, which Luther then went on to hatch. His influence in the thought and literature of the day made the Reformation almost inevitable.

Erasmus (1467-1536) was born the illegitimate son of a priest in Rotterdam. He became an Augustinian priest in 1492, but in 1495 he moved to study in Paris as the life of a

monk did not suit him. His work used satire to ridicule the main trends of his day - **monasticism** and **scholasticism**.

Textbook of the Christian Soldier

This work encouraged lay people to return to the Scriptures and to the teachings of the fathers of the church.

1503

In Praise of Folly

This work expressed his dislike of Rome.

1509

However, all the time he was seeking for a peaceful reform of the Roman church itself, not the establishment of a new church.

On top of all his attacks on the church, Erasmus' greatest role in the Reformation was his edition of the **Greek New Testament**. This was the first of its kind, printed in 1516, the year before the Reformation began.

64

The **Greek New Testament** was used by the Reformers and all who followed them. It critiqued the accepted text, the **Latin Vulgate**, at some critical points. Erasmus also published editions of the church fathers. Erasmus was one of the great **humanists**. That is, someone who argued for a return to the original sources, for the need to study theology in the original languages, so that the church could behave appropriately in his day. **Humanism** was against scholasticism and the authoritarian ideas of the church. For Erasmus, the best way to reform the church was through careful study.

In fact, Erasmus was driven not primarily by his theology, but by his scholarly pursuits.

> GIVEN ALL THIS HE REMAINED A ROMAN CATHOLIC AND WROTE AGAINST LUTHER FOR SPLITTING THE CHURCH.

Erasmus highlighted the importance of looking back to our sources. What are the sources for Christian theology, and how important are they?

The start of the Wars of the Roses	Constantinople is captured by the Ottomans	Richard III becomes King	Columbus reaches America
1453		1483	1492

65

MARTIN LUTHER

Think of the term '**Reformation**' and the name of **Martin Luther** immediately comes to mind. As the period of transformation and of looking back to the sources of the Christian faith progressed, some began to see the church for what it had become. Luther was to be the launch pad for a whole sweep of change.

Brought up in the midst of poverty and religion, **Martin Luther** (1483-1546) was educated at Erfurt University. He became an Augustinian monk, was ordained priest in 1507, and began lecturing in Wittenberg in 1508. He gave lectures on the Bible, and during this period he became concerned about his lack of peace with God. In 1517 he posted the **95 theses** - a list of concerns and worries about the practices of the church - on the church door at Wittenberg. It is this event which is often thought to signal the start of the **Reformation**.

REFORMATION STARTS HERE!

Luther was obsessed with the question of how to be right before God. Central to this question was what the Bible meant by **"the righteousness of God"**. Because God is righteous in himself, God could therefore punish and reward humans according to what they deserved. Yet how could humans ever be called righteous? The righteousness of God is only given to sinful human beings as a gift of God's grace, through the offering of Jesus on the cross.

GRACE

RIGHTEOUSNESS

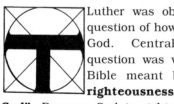

WENT TO CHURCH
TIDIED MY ROOM
GOOD WORKS

FAITH

Hence **justification**, the process of being made righteous, happens by grace through faith alone, rather than through good works or effort.

Luther based this upon his understanding of the difference between **God's law** (for example, the Old Testament laws which make humans aware of their sin and the grace they need) and **God's gospel** (which is an unconditional gift of grace). This was to become the cornerstone of the reformation tradition.

Luther's opposition to the church began in the **95 theses** as an objection to the sale of **indulgences**. This was a way in which people could pay money so that they might be released from some of the temporal punishments for sin given after death.

GIVE ME ANOTHER TENNER AND I'LL GET YOU FORGIVENESS FOR THAT WATER BALLOON YOU THREW AT MR CRITCHLEY

The theses were soon translated and widely distributed. At the beginning of his ministry, Luther wished to stay within the Roman Catholic church and reform it. However, further work...

The Address to the Christian Nobility of the German Nation **and** Freedom of the Christian Man **1520** made his criticisms stronger, and the large gulf between the reformers and the Catholic church began to appear.

Luther attacked the sacramental system of the church, affirming that there were only two proper sacraments (**baptism** and **eucharist**), and he denied the doctrine of transubstantiation and the idea that the mass was a repeat of Christ's sacrifice. In 1521 Luther was excommunicated from the Catholic church.

Canterbury Cathedral completed	Erasmus at Oxford	Henry VIII becomes King
1495	1498	1509

DIET OF WORMS

In 1521 he was brought before the emperor at the **Diet of Worms** and banned. Whilst being hidden by his friends in Wartburg, Luther translated the **New Testament** into the German of the day. As the reformation progressed, many others were to take on the role of reformer. Luther distanced himself from the radicals (in the revolt of the **Peasants' War**, 1525), and in...

At the centre of Luther's thinking was the theology of **the cross**.

attacked some of Erasmus' ideas.

1525

The **Bondage of the Will**

Theology can only take place properly when we see God revealing himself on the cross, not through our own efforts of philosophy and thinking. Luther's whole aim was not to start a new denomination, to split the church, but to return to the **cross of Christ**. He proclaimed,

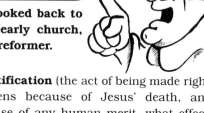

I HAVE TAUGHT YOU CHRIST, PURELY, SIMPLY AND WITHOUT ADULTERATION.

In doing this he looked back to the Bible, to the early church, and so was a true reformer.

If **justification** (the act of being made righteous) happens because of Jesus' death, and not because of any human merit, what effect does this have on our understanding of **the sacraments**? Are they intended to achieve something so that people are made righteous, are they merely a representation of something that has happened elsewhere, or is there something more to them?

The Reformation starts	Henry VIII created Defender of the Faith by Pope	The potato is introduced to Europe
1517	1521	1525

PHILIP MELANCHTHON

The reformation did not happen because of just one person. There were many involved, and

LUTHERANISM

many contributing factors to the rise of **Protestantism** (those who "protested" against the church).

Philip Melanchthon (1497-1560) was to be a natural successor to **Luther**, and a populariser of his work. Educated at Heidelberg and Tübingen, he became a teacher of Greek at **Wittenberg** where he attracted the interest of Luther. So influenced was he by Luther, that he began to study theology.

 He published...

 Common-places of Theology

which was to become an extremely popular textbook of Lutheran theology.

At the **Diet of Augsburg** in 1530 (called by the Roman emperor), Melanchthon presented a list of items believed by the reformers, which is now known as the *Augsburg Confession*. This is now one of the major statements of Lutheranism world-wide, even though some strict Lutherans reject it. It highlighted issues of **justification**,

AUGSBURG the **Trinity**, and condemned various heresies and the extremes of the Anabaptists.

William Tyndale's translation of the New Testament completed

Thomas Cranmer becomes archbishop of Canterbury

1525

1533

To the disappointment of many, Melanchthon compromised with the Catholics later in life. He wished to maintain the peace if at all possible, and opted for a middle way whereby churches were allowed to follow **Protestant doctrine** whilst at the same time keeping **Roman Catholic rituals** and **creeds**. The theological reason for this was that some matters of practice were **"adiaphora"** (matters indifferent), things which were of dispute but not central to the faith. Two prayers are reported of Melanchthon as he died-

THAT THE CHURCHES MAY BE OF ONE MIND IN CHRIST

and that he may be delivered from the...

FURY OF THEOLOGIANS

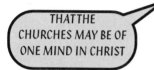

ULRICH ZWINGLI

As Reformation swept across Europe, there were to be other Christian thinkers who would take on board the challenge of reform and adapt it to their own particular situations. Ulrich Zwingli (1484-1531) was born in Switzerland and educated at Basel, Berne, and Vienna. He was ordained a priest in 1506, and had a spell as an army chaplain. In 1519 he became the people's priest in Zurich.

Cranmer annuls Henry's marriage with Catherine of Aragon

Henry marries Anne Boleyn

He is excommunicated from the Catholic church by the Pope

1533

Zwingli was much impressed by the work of Erasmus and his Greek New Testament. He began to be unsure about practices such as the adoration of the saints, and the abuse of the sale of indulgences. His concern was that the church had become unscriptural. It was during these years that he had some sort of conversion experience, and saw the need to speak out against the church.

His regular preaching from the New Testament continued to bring problems to his attention.

He also emphasised the role that ordinary people have in the church, and the need for strong church discipline. He wrote about Scripture, and about **True and False Religion**. His theological emphases were similar to Luther's, especially regarding justification by faith.

Henry becomes Supreme Head of the Church of England	**Miles Coverdale publishes the first complete English Bible**	
1534	1535	

His reforming proposals were perhaps more radical, as were his thoughts on the eucharist. Although he rejected the Lord's supper as a sacrifice, he did not think that the sacrament was merely a memorial. Rather, it enabled the person who had faith to acknowledge the presence of Christ in the act.

Zwingli's life illustrates the importance of factors apart from theology during the reformation. Although accused of heresy by the church, a public council defended Zwingli by taking the area of Zurich out of the bishop's jurisdiction and upholding some of Zwingli's ideas. Thus politics adopted reformation ideas and helped the cause of reform.

Unfortunately Zwingli and Luther continued to drift apart, especially on the issue of the eucharist. At the **Marburg Colloquy** they failed to reach agreement...

I CAN'T POSSIBLY AGREE WITH YOU. YOUR HAT IS CLASHING WITH MINE!

and in 1531 Zwingli was killed after Zurich was captured by Catholic forces. Switzerland was never to be completely reformed as other European countries were, yet Zwingli himself was a great example of the reformers' aims - to bring the church back to its origins, and to organise society on this basis.

The first Act for the dissolution of monastries in England

William Tyndale burned for heresy in the Netherlands

Act of Union unites England and Wales

1536

MARTIN BUCER

Located in Strasbourg, **Martin Bucer** (1491-1551) attempted to bring many of the different parties within the emerging Protestantism together. He attempted to bring **Luther** and **Zwingli** together on the issue of the **eucharist**, to bring **main line reformers** and the **Anabaptists** together, and even to bring **Protestants** and **Catholics** together.

His principles were broadly in line with **Luther**, whilst emphasising the need for an ordered system of **church government** and **discipline**. In addition, he recognised that **civil authorities** had a role to play in the reformation process. Between 1548-51 he taught in Cambridge, and so was to influence the formation of the **_Book of Common Prayer_** and ideas about the relationship between **church** and **state** in England.

Book of Common Prayer

Only recently has Bucer been recognised as an inspiration for the _ecumenical_ movement of today.

Guru Nanak dies (founder of Sikh religion)	Copernicus publishes his work on the cosmos	The _Mary Rose_ sinks
1539	1543	1545

7 3

JOHN CALVIN

John Calvin (1509-64) stands out as one of the pivotal figures of theological history. Bringing together the work of a pastor, theologian, reformer and leader, Calvin influenced not only a city but also a whole religion.

Born in France, Calvin went to school in Paris and studied for both the priesthood and law. He began to appreciate the ideas of the early reformers, and examined the *Greek New Testament*. In about 1535 he experienced some form of sudden conversion, after which he committed himself to the reading and teaching of Scripture along reformation lines.

Between 1538-41 he was involved in pastoral work in Strasbourg, but it was Geneva where he carried out most of his reforming work. Although not a member of the city government, his influence on both church and state was huge.

 Calvin's theology is best known through the writing of his....

In **1536** this started out as a work of 6 chapters,

Institutes of the Christian Religion

BUT BY THE TIME IT APPEARED IN ITS 5TH EDITION IT HAD 79 CHAPTERS.

His foundation was that the Bible is the only source for our knowledge of God. **Revelation** is our only reliable guide. If we look at **nature**, we may find some inkling of God, but this is only partial due to the effects of **the fall**. The task of a theologian is to do justice to the whole of Scripture and to relay a personal encounter with God's word. In Jesus God revealed himself, and in God's self-revelation we see God's glory.

There are many hallmarks of Calvin's theology. He emphasised the God-man nature of Jesus, the way that the Trinity is revealed, and the **glory of God**. Negatively, people have often seen the ideas of **predestination** and **total depravity** as bad aspects of Calvin's theology. As for predestination, Calvin argued that God has decreed who will indeed be saved.

IT'S YOU!

The other side of this is that there are some who will not be saved.

As for total depravity, this is the idea that the fall has made all human beings incapable of any good. What Calvin in fact argued was that the effects of the fall are universal - that is, they apply to everyone, everything, and every area of life. However, this depravity is not *complete* as it is possible for some good to be done.

Calvin was a pastor.

He wanted people to be able to grow up in the faith, and so to be gradually sanctified (made holy) by God's spirit. The doctrine of predestination, and the assurance that this brings, was intended to comfort ordinary people. He was someone who worked hard at the Bible, writing many commentaries and preaching many sermons which illustrated the need to look at the context of each passage, thus contributing to **hermeneutics**.

Calvin was a politician,

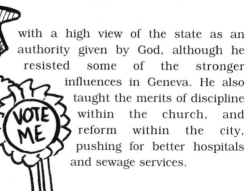

with a high view of the state as an authority given by God, although he resisted some of the stronger influences in Geneva. He also taught the merits of discipline within the church, and reform within the city, pushing for better hospitals and sewage services.

And of course, he was a great theologian.

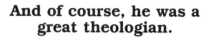

For example, he entered disputes about the **eucharist**, arguing that it was a visible sign of an invisible grace (as **Augustine**), but attacking the extremes of both **transubstantiation** and **mere symbolism**.

After Calvin's death in 1564, his followers carried on his teaching and **Calvinism** began to grow. Many have attempted to get at the heart of his theology, claiming it to be organised around **predestination**, **glory**, **divine sovereignty**, **the fall**, or the **authority of Scripture**.

Ivan the Terrible gains power in Russia	English replaced Latin in English church services	First Book of Common Prayer sanctioned
1547	1549	

YET CALVIN'S GENIUS WAS THE WAY IN WHICH HE HELD THEM TOGETHER, BRINGING TOGETHER THEMES FROM PAUL AND AUGUSTINE. THUS HE PRESENTED AN EXTREMELY ROBUST ARTICULATION OF THE PROTESTANT FAITH.

ROMANS

NTHIANS

e.t.c.

The **Institutes** present a systematic and organised presentation of theology. What are the pros and cons of having a living faith condensed into an ordered list of headings?

I BELIEVE IN A TIN OF BEANS... OH THIS IS MY SHOPPING LIST!

Anabaptist movement reaches England		Catholics persecuted in England	Mary I becomes Queen
1549		1550	1553

7 7

JACOBUS ARMINIUS

The Reformation was not a pure and single event. Many characters led to many disputes. **Jacobus Arminius** (1560-1609) and those who followed him highlighted an important theological controversy that still exists today.

Arminius was a Dutch theologian educated at Marburg, Geneva, Leiden and Basel. From 1603 until his death he was professor at Leiden. He was influenced by a French Protestant theologian, **Theodore Beza**.

It was for his understanding of predestination and free will that Arminius became known. Although he believed in predestination, he was against the idea that the destiny of humans was determined by God prior to the fall.This position implied that the coming of Christ was only a second best plan, because there is then no link between God's decision of who would be chosen, and the coming of Christ to remedy the fall.

SECOND BEST PLAN?

IT S YOU! CAUSE YOU ACCEPT

Arminius argued that God predestines people based on his knowledge of whether they will accept or reject Christ. This is God's foreknowledge.

Thomas Cranmer burned at the stake

Elizabeth I becomes Queen

Plague in London

1556

1558

1563

8
1

The opposing position argued that God's election takes place before the offer of God's grace in Christ, rather than the other way round. It is a completely free act through which God graciously saves, an act not dependent on the human choice of God.

After Arminius' death, **Arminianism** developed to a position of conditional predestination. Humans are predestined, conditional upon their free choice of Christ.

The other implications of what seems like an obscure argument are enormous.

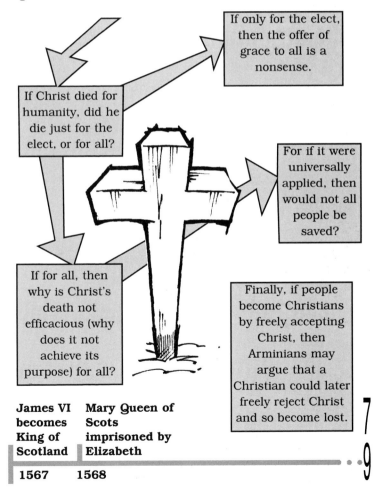

If Christ died for humanity, did he die just for the elect, or for all?

If only for the elect, then the offer of grace to all is a nonsense.

For if it were universally applied, then would not all people be saved?

If for all, then why is Christ's death not efficacious (why does it not achieve its purpose) for all?

Finally, if people become Christians by freely accepting Christ, then Arminians may argue that a Christian could later freely reject Christ and so become lost.

The **Synod of Dort** (1618-19) attempted to deal with these issues, but it ended up condemning the **Remonstrant articles**, those positions which were compiled by Arminius' followers. The Synod replied with what is often labelled **5-point Calvinism**

DORT

1 God sovereignly predestines those who will be saved,

2 the atonement is definite and for those who are predestined (not unlimited in its reach),

3 total depravity affects all humans,

4 God's grace brings about human conversion (not human will),

5 God will persevere with the saints (true Christians cannot fall away).

The Arminians were removed and exiled.

Arminius and the Arminians are examples of how theology can look backwards and forwards. This controversy has hints of the Pelagian controversy of the early church. And later, in the eighteenth century, **John Wesley** took up many of Arminius' points and brought them into the Methodist church.

MENNO SIMONS

Simons (c.1496-1561), although ordained a Catholic priest, became an **Anabaptist** preacher after doubting the doctrines of **transubstantiation** and then **infant baptism**. He was influential amongst the Anabaptists after they suffered a serious defeat at the 1535 **siege of Munster**. Simons wished to base his theology on Scripture alone, and so found no justification for infant baptism. In addition, he urged Christians to be **pacifists**.

ANABAPTISTS WHO ARE THEY?

MANY WELCOMED THE PROTESTANT REFORMATION, BUT SOME STILL THOUGHT THAT WHAT THE MAIN LINE REFORMERS ACHIEVED WAS NOT ENOUGH. KEY ISSUES REVOLVED AROUND THE IDEA OF THERE BEING A **CHURCH LINKED TO THE STATE**, AND THE ISSUE OF **INFANT BAPTISM**. ANABAPTISTS (ANA MEANING AGAIN) INSISTED THAT THE CHURCH CONSISTED OF ONLY TRUE BELIEVERS, AND THE CHURCH MUST SEPARATE ITSELF TO REMAIN PURE. THE **SCLEITHEIM CONFESSION** (1527) REPRESENTS MANY ANABAPTIST IDEAS. THE DESCENDANTS OF **SIMMONS** PARTICULAR BRAND

WHAT? I'M NOT GOING THROUGH THAT AGAIN!

8
1

THE CHURCH IN THE REFORMATION

One of the key issues during this period was the status of **the church**, its structure, and its relationship to the state.

Luther distinguished the **temporal** worldly acts of the state from the **spiritual** acts of the church. However, there are many functions of the church which are non-essential and in which the state can be involved.

Calvin made a stronger break between church and state. The state is given by God to keep the peace and protect the church, but has little role within church affairs. However, there is co-operation of course where church affairs impact on the state.

In the **Church of England**, there developed a very strong relationship between the church and state. Both the **king** and **parliament**, as God-appointed civil authorities, govern the church. The monarch is treated as the head of the church.

In complete contrast to this, the **Anabaptists** advocated complete separation between church and state, for one is completely spiritual, the other temporal. At times this led to disagreement and uprising, and so the Anabaptists were often persecuted for their non-involvement.

Such ideas are still present in certain **Baptist** and **Quaker churches**.

ANABAPTIST

2

IGNATIUS OF LOYOLA

The Catholic church not only reacted against the Reformation, but also produced its fair share of able apologists and theologians. **Ignatius of Loyola** (1491/5-1556) was such a person.

Born to a Spanish nobleman, Ignatius was a professional soldier until he was wounded in 1521. While reading different 'lives of Christ' while recovering, Ignatius resolved to become a soldier for Christ.

Between 1522 and 1523 he spent time praying and drafting his major work, the...

Spiritual Exercises

a set of instructions aimed at developing a Christian's faith.

Whilst studying in Paris, Ignatius and a group of friends vowed to remain celibate and poor, and to set out on a pilgrimage to Jerusalem. Through this the **Society of Jesus** (the **Jesuits**) was born. They swore allegiance to the Pope, and Ignatius became their first general.

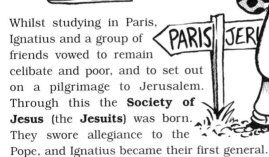

Thirty-nine Articles enacted by Parliament	Beginning of penal legislation against Catholics in England
1571	

86

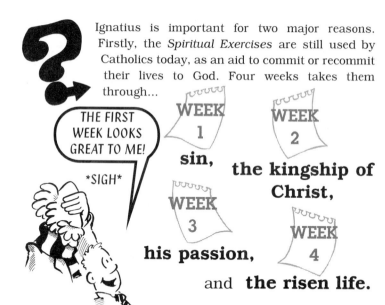

Ignatius is important for two major reasons. Firstly, the *Spiritual Exercises* are still used by Catholics today, as an aid to commit or recommit their lives to God. Four weeks takes them through...

THE FIRST WEEK LOOKS GREAT TO ME!

SIGH

WEEK 1 sin,

WEEK 2 the kingship of Christ,

WEEK 3 his passion,

WEEK 4 and the risen life.

Secondly, the Jesuits have survived until this day, acting as agents for education, apologetics (against Protestants) and mission throughout the world (and are still strong in America, Africa and Asia).

The soldiers of Christ say the following prayer:

TEACH US, GOOD LORD, TO SERVE THEE AS THOU DESERVEST; TO GIVE AND NOT TO COUNT THE COST; TO FIGHT AND NOT TO HEED THE WOUNDS; TO TOIL AND NOT TO ASK FOR REST, TO LABOUR AND NOT TO ASK FOR ANY REWARD SAVE KNOWING THAT WE DO THY WILL, THROUGH JESUS CHRIST OUR LORD.

Ignatius himself is often seen as one of the key figures of the **Catholic Reformation**, or the **Counter Reformation** as it is also known. He, together with the rest of the Jesuits, formed a strong force on which the pope could rely for whatever he wished.

COUNCIL OF TRENT

1545-63

The **Catholic Reformation** was both an inward attempt to deal with some of the problems, and an outward attack against the Protestants. The **Council of Trent** (1545-63) was called by **Pope Paul III** to deal with issues of Reform. It consisted of 3 main sessions, and attracted theologians and priests from across Europe. Some Protestants were allowed, but only to observe.

LOOK DEAR I GOT AN INVITE TO THE COUNCIL OF TRENT!

BUT IT SAYS YOU'RE NOT ALLOWED TO SAY ANYTHING. THAT'LL BE HARD!

INVITE

In essence, the council was a reaffirmation of traditional Roman Catholic teaching. The power of the pope was affirmed, as were the 7 traditional sacraments, the doctrine of transubstantiation, the celibacy of the priesthood, purgatory, and justification by faith *and* works. Indulgences were also affirmed, although the abuses of the sale of them were criticised. All of these issues had been attacked by the reformers at various points. The council was therefore an attempt to restate the case, and to re-enforce the authority and tradition of the Roman Catholic Church. It was not a body for reconciliation, but an attempt to strengthen the church in its own period of reformation. In this it was successful, for Roman Catholics after that time would continually turn back to the council and appeal to its decisions.

85

WILLIAM TYNDALE

Tyndale's influence on English speaking Christianity is huge, due mainly to his translation of the Bible.

Tyndale (c.1494-1536) was educated at both Oxford and Cambridge. As a tutor for a wealthy family, he came to see the ignorance of the clergy around him, and so he was determined to provide as many people as possible with access to the Bible.

DURGH!!

IF GOD SPARE MY LIFE, ERE MANY YEARS SHALL PASS, I WILL CAUSE A BOY THAT DRIVETH THE PLOUGH SHALL KNOW MORE OF THE SCRIPTURES THAN THOU DOST.

The only English translation that existed until his time was that done by **Wycliffe**, yet it was banned as it had been distributed by the **Lollards** who were followers of **Wycliffe**.

THE BIBLE BANNED

8

6 He found little financial support for his project as churchmen feared the influence of **Luther's** ideas at the time.

In 1524 he went to Germany to work on his project in safety, and a year later he was due to go to print when he was raided by the authorities.

Nevertheless, his translation of the **New Testament** was completed, followed by a version of the **Pentateuch**. Copies of both were smuggled into England, but were burnt whenever they were discovered. Tyndale continued to write in support of the **Reformation**, and was eventually caught and burnt at the stake.

RIGHT, THIS ONE'S NEXT!

It is estimated that up to 90 per cent of Tyndale's translation was to form the basis of the later **King James translation** of the Bible. This was foundational not just for the church, but also for the growth of the English language.

YOUR MAJESTY, HERE'S ONE PREPARED EARLIER!

THOMAS CRANMER

One more theologian educated at Cambridge, **Cranmer** (1489-1556) took part in a discussion group held in a pub which examined **Erasmus' Greek New Testament**. From these beginnings he went on to shape the structure of the **Church of England**.

In 1532 he was appointed by **King Henry VIII** as **Archbishop of Canterbury**, the most important bishop in the English church. Although a reluctant archbishop, he suited Henry's purposes as he believed that the monarch's authority was God-given.

TOO RIGHT

In addition, Cranmer was *just* Protestant enough for a King who did not wish to go too far! Henry was not after a great reformer, but someone to see the Church through the continuing battles between the **Roman Catholics** and the **Protestants**. In 1534 Henry enforced the **Act of Supremacy** which severed all links with Rome.

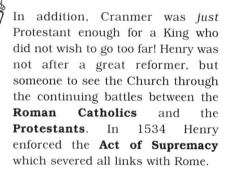

After **Edward VI** came to the throne, Cranmer's achievements included, in 1549, the composition of the first English...

Book of Common Prayer

The first edition was kind to Catholics (for example, **Holy Communion** was referred to as **Mass**), but in its 1552 revision it was unashamedly Protestant.

Francis Drake sets off around the world in the Golden Hind

Colonisation of Ireland begins

1577

1580

This formed the basis for the later 1662...

Book of Common Prayer

a document which has formed the Church of England ever since.

In 1553 Cranmer and **Ridley** (then bishop of London) composed the **42 articles**, later to become the...

39 Articles

the founding document of doctrine for the English church.

When the Catholic **Mary** came to the throne, the Protestants **Latimer** and **Ridley** were burnt at the stake. Cranmer was confused between his Protestant beliefs, and his allegiance to the throne which he thought his faith demanded. Cranmer recanted his Protestant faith, but eventually he was also burnt at the stake. The story is told that as he was preparing to be killed, he placed his right hand (which had signed his recantation) into the fire as a sign that he had gone back on his recantation.

The *Book of Common Prayer* became the most influential book in the English churches, teaching doctrine and faith to all who would go to church. Throughout this and other documents he wrote, Cranmer placed a great stress on the doctrine of **justification by faith** as relevant to everyday life.

Cranmer wished to reform the English church once it was clear that Rome would not itself reform. He believed in the power of the monarch, given by God, and so was caught in a dilemma. Should religion or the state be the ultimate power which we give our allegiance to? Or was Cranmer right in seeking to hold the two together?

39 Articles

Written in 1563, these became the doctrinal standard of Anglican churches around the world. **Cranmer** originally wrote **42** (1553), and although these were suppressed during **Mary's** reign, they then formed the basis for the edition of **39 articles** during **Elizabeth's** reign. They were translated from Latin into English in 1571.

The articles represent an attempt to steer a middle path between Catholicism and Protestantism - **a via media**. Protestant theology was of course paramount. The articles were clear on crucial issues, yet they maintained that beliefs and practices not contrary to what Scripture teaches are allowed. The result of this is that the articles gave the hint of keeping Catholic traditions in mind whilst they followed reformed ideas.

RICHARD HOOKER

When **Mary I** died in 1558, **Elizabeth** came to the throne and brought in the **Elizabethan settlement**. Although some Protestants were not entirely happy, the Queen had gone as far as she had wanted. Some Puritans, who had been in exile in **Geneva** whilst Mary was on the throne, had learnt that the church did not have to be subservient to the state. However, in contrast to this, **Richard Hooker** was one amongst many who saw the Elizabethan situation as ideal.

MARY I RIP

Mary Queen of Scots is executed	Spanish Armada is destroyed	James VI of Scotland becomes James I of England
1587	1588	1603

Hooker (1553/4 - 1600) was born near Exeter, educated in Oxford, and in 1585 moved to **London**. His major work was ...

(it came out in 1661/2 after his death), which argued that the form of the Church of England had many advantages over any other

form of church government. It's arguments followed the thinking of **Aristotle** and **Aquinas**, and drew upon the idea of there being an unchanging natural law. From this he went on to praise the role of the monarch in the Church of England.

In addition, Hooker defended church ceremonies as long as they were not contrary to Scripture and had an authority in either reason or tradition. In opposition to this, some Puritans argued that church practice should only follow what was explicitly taught in the Bible.

Hooker is an important figure when it comes to thinking about authority, tradition, and church government.

HE REPRESENTS A MIDDLE PATH IN THE MIDST OF THE ENGLISH REFORMATION DEBATES.

Authorised Bible published	Pilgrim Fathers arrive in New England	Outbreak of the English Civil War
1611	1620	1642

JOHN OWEN

John Owen (1616-1683) was educated at Queens College, Oxford, and in the 1640s became a minister. He progressed to eventually become vice-chancellor of Oxford University, and to work on **Cromwell's** church system. This proposed that every parish should have an evangelical minister of any Protestant denomination, as long as the minister had been judged worthy by an interdenominational panel. Such a system operated in England until **Charles II** returned to the throne in 1660, when Owen was expelled until his death.

Owen's theology is known for his emphasis on the doctrine of **limited atonement**, as detailed in...

The Death of Death in the Death of Christ

He argued that if the effects of what happened on the cross applied to all human beings, then the atonement is an ineffectual doctrine.

Why? Because this argues that the cross can only *possibly* save people, and no one is therefore guaranteed salvation. However, if limited atonement is true, then only those whom God elects are saved, and this is guaranteed.

LIMITED ATONEMENT

Limited atonement is often accused of being narrow and heartless. That is, only some people are saved by Christ's death, and those not chosen have no hope. In addition, the doctrine of **predestination**, rather than the **cross**, seems to be the controlling idea. However, is there something to recommend such a strong emphasis on the sovereignty of God?

92

JOHN BUNYAN

Born the son of a poor tinker in 1628, **John Bunyan** followed in his father's footsteps before he fought in the Parliamentary army during the **Civil War**.

Bunyan only began to think about what he believed when he married. After his conversion he began to preach at an independent church. However, during this time the British monarchy was restored, and all those who did not accept the Anglican settlement were imprisoned. Bunyan spent over 12 years in a **jail in Bedford**. When offered freedom if he agreed to cease preaching, Bunyan replied,

IF I AM FREED TODAY, I WILL PREACH TOMORROW!

During his imprisonment, Bunyan spent much time writing.

BUNYAN IS MOST WELL KNOWN FOR HIS DEVOTIONAL WRITING, *THE PILGRIM'S PROGRESS*

PILGRIM'S PROGRESS

It tells the story of an everyday Christian life. Modelled on his own experiences, the book has become a widely read and much loved allegory, in which the theological notions of justification, regeneration and sanctification are all portrayed.

Charles 1 executed	**Restoration of Charles II**	**New York founded by the English**
1649	1660	1664

93

He also wrote... **Grace Abounding to the Chief of Sinners** 1665 which was based on his conversion experience.

He died of pneumonia in 1688.

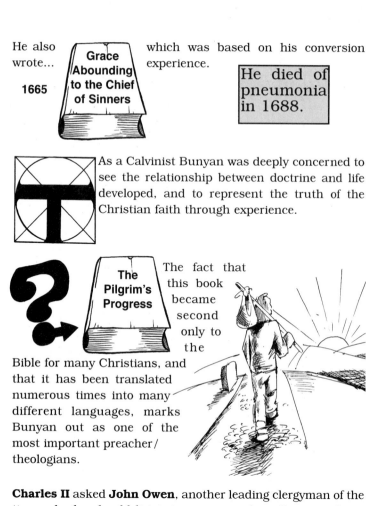

As a Calvinist Bunyan was deeply concerned to see the relationship between doctrine and life developed, and to represent the truth of the Christian faith through experience.

The Pilgrim's Progress

The fact that this book became second only to the Bible for many Christians, and that it has been translated numerous times into many different languages, marks Bunyan out as one of the most important preacher/ theologians.

Charles II asked **John Owen**, another leading clergyman of the time, why he should listen to a man such as Bunyan. Owen replied:

COULD I POSSESS THE TINKER'S ABILITIES FOR PREACHING, PLEASE YOUR MAJESTY, I WOULD GLADLY RELINQUISH ALL MY LEARNING

Great Plague in London	Great Fire of London	James II becomes King	William of Orange lands in England. James flees
1665	1666	1685	1688

JOHN WESLEY

The religious revivals of the eighteenth century are not only important for church history, but also for the theology that they reflect. **John Wesley's** conversion eventually led to the rise of the denomination known as **Methodism**, although like many great theological figures, Wesley's intention was never to start a new movement.

John Wesley (1703-91) was the fifteenth child in a Lincolnshire family. He was educated in **Oxford**, where in 1725 he had his 'religious' conversion from which he intended to make religion his life.

WITH HIS BROTHER CHARLES, JOHN LED A GROUP OF STUDENTS IN OXFORD WHO BECAME KNOWN AS THE "HOLY CLUB" DUE TO THEIR PERSISTENT STUDY, PRAYER, FASTING AND VISITING OF THE SICK.

This was later to be known as **Methodism** due to their disciplined method of Christian living

In 1735 their father died, and the brothers went as missionaries to **Georgia** where they met and were influenced by German **Moravians**.

This was at a **Moravian** meeting in London. At the time he was listening to **Luther's** understanding of **Romans**, and this experience thrust him on into his mission.

 Wesley's stress was on **justification by faith** (from **Luther**) and a personal experience of this in the individual's life. His preaching led to revival in **London**, **Bristol** and elsewhere.

THE ESTAB-LISHED CHURCH THOUGHT THAT HIS PREACHING WAS UNNECESSARY, AND SO THE 'METHODISTS' HAD TO PREACH IN THE OPEN AIR AS THE CHURCHES WERE CLOSED TO THEM.

Methodism centres around the God of love - the fact that everyone can and must be saved by the grace of God drove them into preaching to everyone they could. Wesley himself travelled **4000 miles** each year on horseback in his preaching.

YET THIS WAS NOT CHEAP GRACE, FOR CONVERSION INVOLVES JUSTIFICATION (BEING MADE RIGHT WITH GOD), AND SANCTIFICATION (BEING MADE HOLY)

WORK OF THE HOLY SPIRIT

JUSTIFICATION

SANCTIFICATION

Wesley believed that this regeneration is the progressive ongoing work of the Holy Spirit, yet entire perfection never came in this life. This is against the doctrine of **perfectionism**, the idea that people may become completely holy now, with which Wesley is often accused.

Wesley highlights that theology is no mere academic exercise. His doctrine was based on a relationship with a loving God, a relationship that drove him and others into evangelism, education, production of literature, provision of Sunday Schools, and social concern. In many ways Methodism was **theology at the *coal face***.

THE FOUNDATIONS OF THE ABUNDANT LOVE OF GOD, AND THE IMPORTANCE OF PERSONAL JUSTIFICATION BY FAITH ALONE, LED TO DRAMATIC CHANGES IN THE WAY PEOPLE LED THEIR LIVES.

GEORGE WHITEFIELD

George Whitefield (1714-70) was also converted at Oxford, and became ordained in the Church of England. Involved in the preaching to thousands in England, Scotland, Wales and America, he was a contemporary of **Wesley** and the two knew each other well.

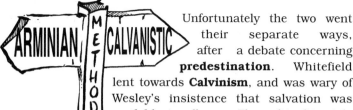

Unfortunately the two went their separate ways, after a debate concerning **predestination**. Whitefield lent towards **Calvinism**, and was wary of Wesley's insistence that salvation was available to *all* now. The split ultimately formed two denominations - **Calvinistic** and **Arminian Methodism**.

Whitefield's unhesitating commitment to the ultimate sovereignty of God combined itself with an offer of salvation to those who would believe. His desire was not to lead a form of Methodism, and he is remembered by the phrase,

LET THE NAME OF WHITEFIELD PERISH, BUT LET CHRIST BE GLORIFIED!

Anne becomes Queen	Union of Scotland and England	Office of Prime minister introduced	Beginning of Methodist revival
1702	1707	1721	1729

JONATHAN EDWARDS

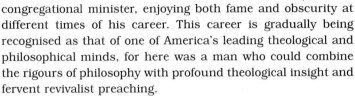

The religious awakenings in **America** during the eighteenth century were characterised by the leading and thinking of one great man, **Jonathan Edwards** (1703-58). Brought up in a Christian home, and having studied at **Yale University**, Edwards became a congregational minister, enjoying both fame and obscurity at different times of his career. This career is gradually being recognised as that of one of America's leading theological and philosophical minds, for here was a man who could combine the rigours of philosophy with profound theological insight and fervent revivalist preaching.

 Edwards was a **strict Calvinist**, who believed that certain beliefs could be proved - such as that an eternal cause of the universe exists. However, even if reason can prove so much, without God's **self-revelation** human beings are left in the dark for they are...

NATURALLY BLIND IN THE THINGS OF RELIGION.

Why so blind? Primarily because of the affects of the **fall**, resulting in **sin**. Edwards was able to draw all his theology from Scripture, and at the same time enter into dialogue with the likes of **John Locke** and **Isaac Newton**.

State of Georgia founded

1732

Start of the Jacobite Rebellion

1745

Central to Edwards' thought was the **glory of God**. Creation was an act of his glory, and the end of God's grace in Christ was also his glory.

The Freedom of the Will — 1754

and

Original Sin — 1758

spelled out his thought on the relationship of humans to God. Free will is not some independent action, but when someone wills something they then act in accordance with their character.

Edward's aim was to attack any view of **free will** that undermined either the created order or the sovereignty of God. Although appearing theoretical, Edwards' theology was extremely practical. Even though he agreed with Enlightenment thinkers that human beings can recognise morality, he criticised this morality for being purely self-interested. Rather, true virtue consists in loving God, and such love must then be expressed practically.

Among other matters, Edwards raised the question of free will. What do we mean by free will? Are we free to do whatever we wish, or are there restrictions on our freedom? And if God is sovereignly in charge, how much of our will is down to us, and how much down to God?

YOU ARE NOW FREE TO CHOOSE TO DO WHAT EVER YOU WANT.

Settlers first arrive in Tennessee **North Dakota first settled** **Start of American War of Independence**

1757   1766   1775

The period of the Reformation and beyond was a turning point in both history and theology.

Culture,

society,

language,

government,

and many other aspects of life were changed

THEOLOGY WAS FORCED TO LOOK BACK TO ITS SOURCES, AND TO ASK FUNDAMENTAL QUESTIONS ABOUT WHAT IT MEANS TO BE A CHRISTIAN.

The face of Christian theology has never been the same since, with a permanent divide between **Catholicism** and **Protestantism** being fixed.

Only in recent years, in the modern era, have there been moves towards reconciliation between these two and the many other denominations within the church.

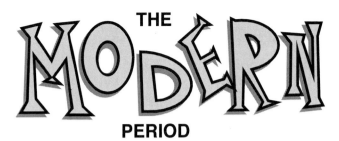

THE MODERN PERIOD

The history of theology has shown that great changes have taken place at various points in time. Perhaps the greatest shift was to occur in the last few centuries.

Key philosophers (for example, Descartes and Kant) challenged the way we think, and so how theology is done.

Others would attack foundational beliefs (Darwin)

or the way that we approach the search for God (Freud and Marx).

Biblical specialists would question the historical reliability of the Bible (Harnack),

and others would criticise the whole basis on which theology was done (feminist and liberation theologians).

In addition, the world would see some of the worst examples of evil and destruction it would ever know (two world wars, and the Holocaust).

IN THE MIDST OF ALL THIS, MANY OF THE SAME THEOLOGICAL QUESTIONS AND ISSUES REMAINED. MODERN THEOLOGY REMAINS A FASCINATING PERIOD, AND A GREAT RESOURCE FOR THE JOURNEY OF THEOLOGY.

IMMANUEL KANT

Although not a theologian, **Kant** (1724-1804) and his thought was significant for the development of modern theology. His philosophical reflections were to influence most areas of theology. Born the son of a saddler, he became a professor of logic in east Prussia. He is now viewed as a leading figure of the **Enlightenment**, a period of history which saw a drastic and speedy change in the way that people viewed the world.

THE ENLIGHTENMENT WAS AN AGE WHEN PEOPLE SAW THE IMPORTANCE OF REASON, AND BEGAN TO CHALLENGE THE THOUGHT AND TRADITIONS THAT HAD BEEN PASSED ON TO THEM.

"Epistemology" refers to how we know things, how human beings can have knowledge.

Empiricism taught that we could have knowledge only through our senses, through what we could see, touch, experience.

Rationalism taught that knowledge came through thinking, through reason.

SNIFF SNIFF! DROOL! SLOBBER! etc

REASON

Storming of the Bastille	The 'Reign of Terror'
1789	1793

In both 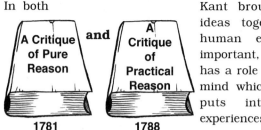 Kant brought these two ideas together. Although human experiences are important, the mind also has a role to play. It is the mind which classifies and puts into order our experiences.

In fact, Kant believed that humans are unable to know things in themselves. What we do know is our experience of these things.

EXPERIENCE THIS!

What this means for God is that we cannot have knowledge of God in himself. Reason does not help here, because any attempt to prove God's existence must fail.

How then can theology work? For Kant, what matters is a practical faith.

The other implication of Kant's work which influences theology is in the realm of ethics. Human reason is the source of morality, yet in order to make moral judgements we must presume that God exists.

FRIEDRICH SCHLEIERMACHER

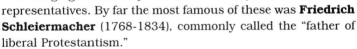

One of the major movements within modern theology was known as **liberal Protestantism**. Like any movement it was wide-ranging, had many facets, and many representatives. By far the most famous of these was **Friedrich Schleiermacher** (1768-1834), commonly called the "father of liberal Protestantism."

Schleiermacher was converted through the Moravian church, and his background was influenced by the likes of Kant, Plato, and by movements such as the Reformation, Romanticism and Pietism.

Like many theologians, his desire was to reconstruct the Christian faith for his time. This was a job he attempted through many works, most important of which were...

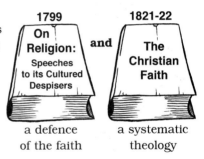

1799
On Religion:
Speeches to its Cultured Despisers

and

1821-22
The Christian Faith

a defence of the faith

a systematic theology

Schleiermacher taught at Halle and Berlin.

Two aspects of Schleiermacher's thought are central.

FIRSTLY, THE CONVICTION THAT THEOLOGY MUST BE RELATED TO THE CHURCH COMMUNITY. THIS GAVE SCHLEIERMACHER HIS DRIVE TO RELATE EVERYTHING TO THE SITUATION OF THE DAY, AND HIS CONCERN WITH HERMENEUTICS.

SECONDLY, AND MORE FUNDAMENTALLY, WAS SCHLEIERMACHER'S BELIEF THAT THEOLOGY SHOULD BE GROUNDED IN FEELING AND EXPERIENCE (RATHER THAN TRADITIONAL SOURCES OF AUTHORITY).

Within everyone there is a consciousness of God, an awareness of something ultimate, which is just waiting to be awakened.

Following on from this then, theology is not mere words or beliefs. Rather, religion is....

THE CONSCIOUSNESS OF BEING ABSOLUTELY DEPENDENT, OR, WHICH IS THE SAME THING, OF BEING IN RELATION WITH GOD.

Hegel joked that because of this relationship between dependence and religion, a dog must therefore be more religious than its master, as it is the more dependent one!

WOOF

However, Schleiermacher simply meant that this feeling of absolute dependence demonstrates that no one is self-sufficient, that there is something greater than the world holding it together. How does this relate to Christianity? Christianity is the best expression of this consciousness.

CHRISTIANITY

This system moved beyond the boundaries that Kant and others had put on religion. Religion is now not just about knowing and doing, but is to do with the very bedrock of reality. The implications for this approach are numerous.

Religious devotion becomes central to the Christian life. Revelation comes through the *experiences* of the church and the experiences of the New Testament (not the *words* in the New Testament).

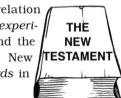

THE NEW TESTAMENT

Schleiermacher's theology had a low view of human sinfulness, and hence a low view of Christ's work on the cross. Sin is reinterpreted as resistance to God-consciousness, and salvation is the awakening of this consciousness. Who is Jesus then? He is the archetype of God-consciousness, entering into sympathy with the human situation, and spreading God-consciousness to all who believe in him.

SYMPATHY WITH HUMAN SITUATION

Was Schleiermacher forming a purely subjective religion? Barth accused him of reducing theology to the merely human level. Yet Schleiermacher's emphasis on the subjective is an important part of Christian experience, and his concept of the feeling of dependence does refer to something external, not just to mere feelings. Schleiermacher may have been too preoccupied with human experience, but his theology attempted to defend the Christian faith to the critics of his time.

Napoleon seizes power in France	Ireland becomes part of the United Kingdom	Battle of Trafalgar
1799	1801	1805

SØREN KIERKEGAARD

Existentialism is another movement which is huge and hard to define. Within its stream, **Soren Kierkegaard** (1813-55) developed a form of Christian existentialism, and was to have a profound effect on modern theology.

Kierkegaard was Danish, the son of a Lutheran, who lived in Copenhagen. His father influenced him heavily throughout his upbringing, bringing to Kierkegaard a profound struggle with guilt. In his lifetime Kierkegaard broke off an engagement which he felt was similar to Abraham's willingness to sacrifice Isaac, and hence a demonstration of what it means to be an authentic disciple of Christ.

The earnest aim of Kierkegaard was to show what Christianity really was, to reintroduce real life Christian faith to a dead Christendom. One of his main concerns was with the nature of faith. Faith is not something you can have by being a 'name' Christian. Faith is not purely something intellectual.

RATHER, FAITH IS ABOUT ETHICAL ACTION AND PRACTICAL STEPS. EVEN MORE SO, FAITH IS ABOUT AN INDIVIDUAL, FOR EACH PERSON IS ACCOUNTABLE BEFORE GOD, EACH ONE HAS TO TAKE THESE STEPS THEMSELVES.

110

What are the steps of faith?

Christian faith is **"the task of becoming subjective"**, that is actually being involved in **struggle**, in **decision**, and in **action**.

STRUGGLE   DECISION   ACTION

Kierkegaard was horrified that people thought they could acquire truth from others. Rather, a Christian is a person who is passionately involved in God and made aware of their sin.

WITHIN THIS SYSTEM, JESUS IS THE ONE **(THE INFINITE QUALITATIVE DIFFERENCE)** WHO BRIDGES THE GULF BETWEEN HUMAN BEINGS AND GOD. HE ADDRESSES INDIVIDUALS NOW. HE IS THE TRUTH WHICH WE HAVE TO GET HOLD OF.

HUMAN KIND   GOD

In Jesus, God appears **'incognito'**, for the normal eye cannot see God in Jesus, but the eye of faith can.

Kierkegaard's stress on individualism and hence separation from the church led to periods of serious self-doubt, something he regarded as the mark of true faith.

THAT'S RIGHT, THE MARK OF TRUE FAITH... I THINK... WELL MAYBE IT'S NOT... OH I REALLY DON'T KNOW.

Once he was made a laughing stock due to some comments he made in a paper, yet for Kierkegaard this was the price paid for being a true believer.

Thus Kierkegaard did not change Christianity like the **liberal Protestants** to make it easier to swallow, but affirmed Christianity as offensive.

The existential thrust of his work focused on the subjective, on the individual person. Yet this was not to put humans above God, but so that they could encounter God and be made a true person. A famous expression of his thought is...

"TRUTH IS SUBJECTIVITY."

This does not mean there is no substance to Kierkegaard's theology. Rather, that the truth that matters is seized with passion inwardly - faith involves risk, personal involvement, and knowing God through loving him (not loving God through knowing about him). Kierkegaard therefore went against much of what was around in his day. His work was to influence **Barth**, **Bultmann**, **Heidegger** & **Sartre**.

CHARLES FINNEY

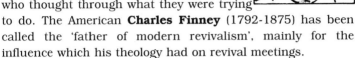

We may not immediately think of revivals when we think of theologians. However, these events of church history involve people who thought through what they were trying to do. The American **Charles Finney** (1792-1875) has been called the 'father of modern revivalism', mainly for the influence which his theology had on revival meetings.

Finney trained as a lawyer, and after a conversion experience in 1821 he was ordained as a minister in the Presbyterian church in 1824. In his life he was an evangelist who travelled the world, a professor of theology at Oberlin College in Ohio, a pastor, and a college president.

Finney was quite radical in that he argued that revivals could actually be promoted. Against the prevailing Calvinistic thought of his day, he argued that human beings had an important part to play in their conversion. Repentance, according to Finney, is an act of the will which human beings can bring about without having to sit around 'waiting' for God to act. Finney's theology was to be known as 'New School Calvinism', and included the teaching that human nature and society could be made perfect.

NEW SCHOOL CALVINISM

PERFECT RESULTS!

George III dies	The first police force introduced in London	George IV dies
1820	1829	1830

Underlying his thinking was the denial of original sin as taught by the Calvinists, and the conviction that moral action is an isolated free act of the will.

This means that when we come to make a decision, all we have to do is decide - there is nothing else, like our moral character and the people we have become, that acts upon these decisions.

Finney's theology has been extremely influential on American evangelicalism, and his thoughts about preparing for revival have been taken to extremes in some circles.

CHARLES HADDON SPURGEON

Born in Essex, **Spurgeon** (1834-1892) is remembered more as a great Baptist preacher who drew thousands to listen to him, than as a theologian. After a dramatic conversion, his theology was evangelical and Calvinist, and he helped to influence the spread of evangelicalism in reaction to liberalism. His theology also lead him to be strongly involved in politics and social action.

BENJAMIN WARFIELD

Evangelicals represent a significant proportion of Christians world-wide. This may not have always been represented by the theological world, but there is an increasing realisation that evangelical theology has to be taken seriously. Warfield was one theologian at the forefront of modern evangelicalism and its reaction against liberalism.

Benjamin Warfield (1851-1921) was educated at Princeton seminary in America, under the influence of what was known as Scottish Common Sense philosophy.

After graduating he married, and eventually taught New Testament and then theology at Princeton. Early in their married life his wife became ill, and so he spent many of his years caring for her at the same time as developing his theology.

Warfield followed the Calvinism of Charles Hodge (who was one of the first teachers at Princeton), and never moved to the New School Calvinism which Finney developed. His main work was to defend traditional doctrine against liberalism, and his most influential writings concerned the doctrine of Scripture.

William IV dies	The potato famine in Ireland
1837	1846

Essay on Inspiration

1881

written with A A Hodge, reacted against the higher critical views of Scripture which the liberals had developed. Warfield argued that the Scriptures themselves witnessed to the fact that they were inspired by God, and so the original manuscripts of the Bible were without error. Divine inspiration of the Bible writers did not mean that the Bible was merely dictated, but that God worked through their humanity. In this way the words of the writers became the very words of God and so were infallible.

Warfield also criticised the different views on spirituality that existed during his lifetime - both the romantic liberal spiritual life, and the revivalist religious life which flourished.

Warfield's doctrine of Scripture remains influential amongst evangelicals. He and others provided the backdrop to a project which appeared between 1910 and 1915. Called...

The Fundamentals

they were a series of booklets that answered the criticisms of liberalism, and set the agenda for evangelicalism and fundamentalism in the following years.

Such an understanding of the inspiration of Scripture is often accused of ignoring the human nature of the texts we have. Does this not turn the human writers into a typewriter used by God? However, if we stress the human nature too much, do we end up with a Bible which we can neither trust nor obey?

THE BIBLE
Part 1

JOHN HENRY NEWMAN

In the midst of the Victorian age, with the growth of both **liberalism** and **evangelicalism**, a movement began that emphasised the **Catholicism** of the Anglican theological tradition. **John Henry Newman** (1801-1890) was a key player in this **Oxford Movement**, and was noted for his move into the Roman Catholic Church.

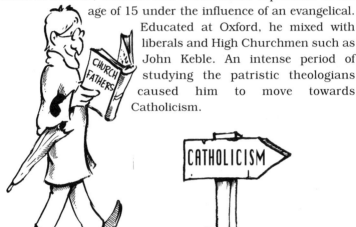

Born in London, Newman had a conversion experience at the age of 15 under the influence of an evangelical. Educated at Oxford, he mixed with liberals and High Churchmen such as John Keble. An intense period of studying the patristic theologians caused him to move towards Catholicism.

Whilst he was vicar at St Mary's, Oxford, he resigned from his position in 1843 and was accepted into the Church of Rome in 1845. Two years later he was ordained a priest in Rome, and then returned to work in Birmingham for the rest of his life.

The Crimean War begins

The charge of the Light Brigade

1854

7

Newman's name will always be linked with thinking about the church and its authority - that is, ecclesiology.

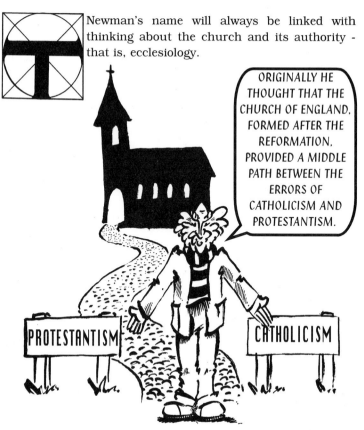

ORIGINALLY HE THOUGHT THAT THE CHURCH OF ENGLAND, FORMED AFTER THE REFORMATION, PROVIDED A MIDDLE PATH BETWEEN THE ERRORS OF CATHOLICISM AND PROTESTANTISM.

PROTESTANTISM

CATHOLICISM

Yet he gradually changed his mind, and was more comfortable with the idea that the Church of Rome represented the true line of the church, from St Peter onwards.

In **1845** he published an...

Essay on the Development of Christian Doctrine

Not only did this justify his conversion to Rome, but he explored the idea that Christian doctrine can develop. Such an idea was not necessarily new. However how could one decide what was a legitimate development, and what was false. Outlining several criteria, Newman realised that such a system would need an authoritative and regulative interpreter. For Newman this guide to interpreting the development of doctrine was the Church of Rome.

Nevertheless, Newman was uncomfortable with the idea that the Pope was infallible, that he could not make a mistake, even though such a belief was affirmed at the first Vatican Council.

1ST VATICAN COUNCIL

Newman thought that others should be consulted, and that church structures should be more creative. It was for these views that the authorities in Rome considered him to be the most dangerous man in England!

Newman's thoughts on ecclesiology had some influence in the Oxford Movement, but in reality they never achieved much recognition until this century.

Some have described the second Vatican Council as Newman's council, for here his theology was recognised as bringing important ideas about the church to light.

2ND VATICAN COUNCIL

Other contributions by Newman included an...

which analysed religious belief and how it grows, and...

examining the place of theology in a university education.

Darwin announces his theory of Evolution

SIGMUND FREUD

Known to most people, **Sigmund Freud** (1856-1939) was not a theologian, but his thought was to have great impact on the study of religion and theology. The person behind modern psychoanalysis, Freud's attack on Christian theology was particularly severe.

Freud was born a Jew in Moravia into a family of 8, and financial pressure led to train as a doctor. Involved in the treatment of patients with neuroses, Freud began to experiment with hypnosis and free association, examining human instincts and subconscious. He went on to develop his theories of psychoanalysis, proposing different levels of human consciousness which affect everyday life.

Freud was impressed by Darwin's theories, and had great faith in science's ability to do away with religious explanations.

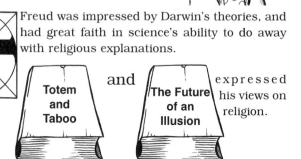

Totem and Taboo and **The Future of an Illusion** expressed his views on religion.

1913   1927

Christianity is basically wish-fulfilment. It is an illusion from which humans need rescuing. All religions could be classed as 'the universal obsessional neurosis of humanity'. No God really existed, it was merely something we wished to exist, to cope with our situation.

Florence Nightingale founds training school for nurses

The American Civil War begins

1860   1861

Why was Freud convinced of this? He was convinced that during childhood, sexuality is repressed, with disastrous consequences.

OK I DON'T WANT YOU TO BE THINKING ABOUT **SEX**, GOT IT? I WANT YOU TO SCRUB THOSE THREE LITTLE LETTERS FROM YOUR MIND... **S.E.X**. IF I EVEN CATCH YOU MENTIONING **SEX**...

These desires are then projected onto a God-like figure, in order to cope with insecurities that have arisen from childhood.

As an illusion, Freud thought Christian theology was dangerous, something that people needed to wake up to and be rescued from. His theories on religion, along with those on sexuality and psychoanalysis, were to have a huge impact during the twentieth century. Darwin, Marx and Freud together presented an enormous challenge to all traditional theology, and caused many to doubt their Christian convictions.

Without being able to evaluate Freud's theory about the origin of religion, is it possible to still criticise him for the logical step he makes? That is, even though he may have identified the human source of religious belief, does this necessarily mean that God does not exist?

The transportation of criminals to Australia ends

Zulu War in Southern Africa

1868

1879

ADOLF VON HARNACK

Liberal Protestantism became a major force within theology and within the church. **Adolf von Harnack** (1851-1930) contributed to its spread, and became one of its most important spokesmen. Originally a church historian who taught at Leipzig, Marburg and Berlin, von Harnack's work took him into systematic theology and biblical studies.

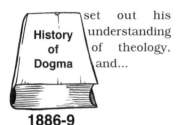

History of Dogma set out his understanding of theology, and...

1886-9

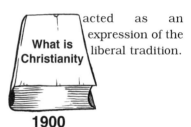

What is Christianity acted as an expression of the liberal tradition.

1900

In his study of the history of doctrine, von Harnack concluded that Christianity had been developed by Paul and then Catholicism in such a way that it distorted the original and much more practical thrust of Jesus' teaching. Alien Greek thought forms had intruded into the pure gospel.

WHAT THEOLOGIANS SHOULD DO IS DISCARD THIS GREEK HUSK WHICH IS A PRODUCT OF A PARTICULAR TIME AND PLACE, IN ORDER TO GET AT THE TRUE KERNEL OF THE FAITH. THIS KERNEL IS PERMANENTLY VALID, AND VON HARNACK IDENTIFIED THE KERNEL WITH JESUS' TEACHING ON THE KINGDOM OF GOD.

122

Von Harnack also ventured into the study of the New Testament, reconstructing a hypothetical text known simply as Q which is thought to lie behind the Synoptic gospels, and expressing a conservative view by giving an early date for the composition of the Synoptic gospels. He also specialised in the study of patristic theology.

The model of the husk and kernel had radical implications for traditional Christianity. According to Harnack, the Trinity and the incarnation were...

THE FRUIT OF THE GREEK SPIRIT ON THE GROUND OF THE GOSPEL.

This must now be eliminated, for Jesus' message concerned only the Father, not the Son. Although Jesus embodied his own message, he taught nothing about incarnation and Trinity. Rather, the emphasis is on ethical teaching, especially the fatherhood of God, the brotherhood of men and women, and the infinite value of the human soul.

Von Harnack's influence on the study of the New Testament is considerable. Perhaps his attempt at getting rid of the husk of Christianity went too far. Nevertheless, his stress on the ethical teaching of the gospel was one amongst many important contributions. In the light of all of this, is it surprising that von Harnack had considerable sympathies with Marcion?

The first Boer War begins	**Queen Victoria's Golden Jubilee**	**The first underground railway in London**
1880	1887	1890

ALBERT SCHWEITZER

Theology is littered with brilliant minds, and **Albert Schweitzer** (1875-1965) was certainly one of those. Born in Alsace, he was a philosopher, a theologian, a musician, and a doctor! He ended his days as a missionary doctor in Africa, where he even constructed his own hospital.

His major contribution to theology was an analysis of liberal attempts to reconstruct the life of Jesus.

In...

The Quest of the Historical Jesus

1906

Schweitzer argued that all these reconstructions were simply the life of Jesus rewritten with Protestant liberalism added. They all reflected the author's own liberal theology.

Instead of this historical attempt at understanding Jesus, Schweitzer proposed that the key was eschatological. That is, Jesus' teaching was all about the end times, about the coming kingdom of God.

BEHOLD THE KINGDOM OF GOD IS AT HAND!

Queen Victoria dies	Baden-Powell founds the Boy Scout movement	Edward VII dies	Amundsen beats Scott to the South Pole
1901	1908	1910	1911

Jesus' proposal was that he and all his disciples should die and bring in this kingdom. In actual fact, Jesus died on behalf of his disciples, and Paul then thought that the kingdom had come, even though this kingdom was invisible.

JESUS PREACHED AN 'INTERIM' ETHIC, ONE GIVEN FOR THE TIME BETWEEN HIS COMING AND THE COMING OF THE KINGDOM.

THE KINGDOM IS AT HAND

YOU ARE HERE

THE END

This teaching was basically reverence for life, all life whether animals, plants, insects, or others. Schweitzer went on to develop this line of thinking in much of his work.

Schweitzer has been criticised by liberals for his attack on their theology, and by conservatives for his interpretation of the life of Jesus, but his helpful contribution was to show the difficulties which much of liberalism had got itself into.

GUSTAF AULÉN

The doctrine of the atonement (what theologians understand happens on the cross) is crucial to theology. In fact, using the word 'crucial' is slightly strange, since the word comes from the Greek for "cross". Something is crucial because it is central to everything, just as the cross is central to Christian theology. It is for his views on the atonement that **Gustaf Aulén** (1879-1977) is most well known.

As both a professor of theology and a bishop in the Swedish church, Aulén was one of the most important Scandinavian theologians of the modern age.

He contributed to the ecumenical project in trying to bring churches of different traditions together, as well as promoting Lutheran studies. In much of his theology he held ideas similar to neo-orthodoxy, that stream of theology which followed Barth.

His most important work...

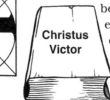

Christus Victor

...began life as a course of lectures examining the meaning of the cross. Aulén attempted to correct the difference between the objective and the subjective understandings of the atonement.

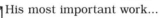

The Titanic sinks	World War II begins	The first tanks used in battle	The USA enters the war
1912	1914	1916	1917

Objective theories said that, in some way, Jesus took the place of humanity so that the punishment which had been due to them was taken instead by Jesus on the cross.

Subjective theories tended to say that the death of Jesus was given as an example to humanity.

Between these two ends of the spectrum, Aulén put forward what he called the 'classic' view of the atonement. This is that what took place on the cross was the result of a divine conflict between God and the forces of evil. On the cross God triumphs over evil, death, and sin.

AULÉN TRACED THIS VIEW OF THE ATONEMENT FROM THE NEW TESTAMENT, THROUGH IRENAEUS AND LUTHER, AND ARGUED THAT IT NEEDED TO BECOME MORE WIDESPREAD IN HIS DAY.

His views were well received, probably because of the century in which he was writing where world wars had made it very clear that forces of evil were at work.

The classic view of the atonement paints a picture of another important understanding of this doctrine, and reminds theologians that there are different interpretations that might not necessarily exclude one another.

There are many different ways of representing what happened on the cross, from a victory, to an example, and to the language of satisfaction and substitution.

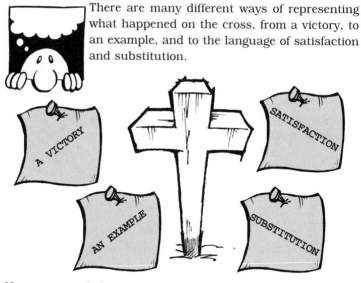

A VICTORY

SATISFACTION

AN EXAMPLE

SUBSTITUTION

However, was Aulen mistaken to see them as all rival views, or may it be possible to see some or all of them representing part of the truth?

Ireland is divided into North and South	Alexander Fleming discovers penicillin	Amy Johnson flies from England to Australia
1921	1928	1930

RUDOLF BULTMANN

A whole century of biblical studies and theology was influenced by the work of **Bultmann**. His existential interpretation of the Christian faith was to challenge many firmly held conclusions, in an attempt to bring theology alive to new generations.

New Testament

Bultmann (1884-1976) studied at Marburg, Tübingen and Berlin. His teaching positions included a thirty year stint as Professor of New Testament at Marburg from 1921 until 1951, and his major contribution was to the study and theology of the New Testament.

Bultmann's concern was to enable modern men and women to read the New Testament, even though it was written in a world many centuries apart from ours.

His influence was so great that his major work...

Theology of the New Testament

is still referred to today.

1948

Bultmann is associated with the term demythologisation. That is, Bultmann recognised that the Bible was written in the context of a supernatural world which no longer makes any sense to us today. The New Testament contains important teaching about the human situation, which is known as the *kerygma*, the message. Yet this is written in mythological language which needs to be properly interpreted.

129

Therefore, Bultmann started a process of demythologising the New Testament, interpreting the texts in their proper way. A myth is not something which is necessarily 'untrue', but rather an expression of something real about human experience.

The History of the Synoptic Tradition

1921

represented an extremely sceptical approach to the history of the New Testament. Bultmann believed that the Gospels contained very little historical information about Jesus, but rather information about how the early Christian communities understood Jesus. Therefore the term "the Christ of Faith", rather than "the Jesus of History", became associated with Bultmann.

Yet Bultmann did not follow this path because he wanted to be sceptical for its own sake. He stressed the importance of an existential encounter with God, rather than mere historical knowledge. What matters is the decision of faith in response to the *kerygma*. In this way he believed he followed the line of Luther. Luther threw out dependence on human works and emphasised justification by faith. Bultmann also threw out the dependence of human beings on historical knowledge, emphasising the faith response.

Although Bultmann had a commendable aim of explaining the faith, was he wrong to make history almost irrelevant? Indeed, New Testament historians since Bultmann have shown that there is a much more secure historical basis for what we know of Jesus than Bultmann allowed.

Nazis take power in Germany	George V dies	Edward VIII abdicates	Southern Ireland becomes independent
1933	1936		1937

KARL BARTH

The face of theology in the twentieth century was permanently changed by the contribution of this Swiss theologian. One of the greatest theologians of the modern age, **Barth** represents a major critical response to the enlightenment and to the theology of liberalism.

Barth was born a Swiss, studied in Tubingen and Marburg, and was taught by, among others, von Harnack. Between 1911 and 1921 he was a pastor in Safenwil, Switzerland, where gradually the trials of war and his frustrations at liberal theology took its toll. The problem was, liberalism could not tell Barth what to teach his congregation Sunday by Sunday.

In **1919** Barth published his...

Central to this was an emphasis on the sovereignty of God, a God who is 'wholly other' - completely different to what we can ever imagine.

Commentary on Romans

revised 1922

Barth became heavily involved in the Confessing Church in Germany which rejected the rule of the Nazis, and Barth was the chief author behind the **Barmen Declaration** (1934) which opposed Hitler, for which Barth was dismissed from Germany and forced to return to Basel.

Germany invades Poland

1939

131

The theme of the work on Romans was "the Godness of God", the belief that there is a radical difference between God and humanity, and that religion all too often forgets this. God is God, not man (or woman) writ large.

Together with this emphasis on the otherness of God, Barth attacked religion as a human construct. Any form of religion is an attempt to domesticate God, to put him in a box, or even to run away from God.

Christianity, in contrast, is a revelation from God to which people can respond.

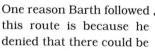

Early in Barth's life he was known for his **'dialectical'** theology, that is contrasting paradoxical themes within theology to make a point. On the cross we see God's 'No', his condemnation of sin, and God's 'Yes', when Christ is raised from the dead.

One reason Barth followed this route is because he denied that there could be any single concept by which we could grasp God. Additionally, there was no 'analogy of being' between God and humanity, no likeness that we could use to describe God and say, for example, his love is like our love but better. All that we know about God comes from revelation.

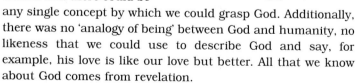

	The Japanese attack Pearl Harbor and the USA joins the war	The Allies invade Europe
The Battle of Britain		
1940	1941	1944

132

Much of Barth's efforts went into writing the massive...

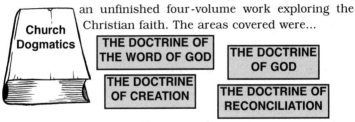

an unfinished four-volume work exploring the Christian faith. The areas covered were...

Church Dogmatics

| THE DOCTRINE OF THE WORD OF GOD | THE DOCTRINE OF GOD |
| THE DOCTRINE OF CREATION | THE DOCTRINE OF RECONCILIATION |

At it's heart, the *Church Dogmatics* were about Jesus Christ and his act of bridging the gulf between God and human beings. For Barth, Christology was the key on which everything turns.

The centrality of Christ in Barth's theology meant that he was hostile to any attempts to base theology on human reason. This also led to a debate with **Emil Brunner** on the role of natural theology. Barth denied any role for such thinking, as the direction of theology should be from the divine to the created, not from creation to the divine. However, Brunner was prepared to admit that there are some things we can learn outside of revelation. Both theologians have been labelled as **'neo-orthodox'**, but they eventually followed different paths over this issue. Barth said that he and Brunner were like the elephant and the whale - both were God's creatures, but they were destined to never meet!

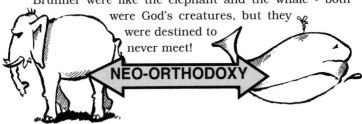

NEO-ORTHODOXY

Barth's whole attitude was therefore in strict opposition to that of Schleiermacher and other liberals. Schleiermacher was concerned with religion, Barth was concerned with the Word of God as revealed. In effect, Barth's contribution was to reorientate theology around the centre of Christ.

3

Barth's contribution was enormous. He has influenced many theologians, including the likes of **Jungel** and **T F Torrance**. Yet others, such as **Pannenberg**, have argued that Barth is so confident in the self-evidence of theology that he is guilty of the charge of **fideism**, distrusting reason and making faith a leap in the dark (the influence of Kierkegaard is clearly seen). Again, if the work of Christ is emphasised to such an extent, is there any real place left for freedom, sin and rebellion? Others have charged Barth with lacking a proper doctrine of the Spirit. However, we may say

that Barth's theology is too much from above, not practical enough, or too ontological, yet with such a massive contribution we must be careful of missing much of what this great theologian had to say.

BARMEN DECLARATION

Written in 1934, this was put together by Germans within the 'Confessing' Church who were opposed to the Nazi 'German-Christian' movement. This movement was characterised by extreme nationalism and anti-Semitism. The Declaration involved the likes of Bonhoeffer and Barth, and stressed the authority of Christ and the Scriptures. Most importantly, the declaration challenged the attempt to place the church under the authority of the state.

Atomic bombs are dropped on Japan	**Led by Gandhi, India becomes independent**	**George VI dies**
1945	1947	1952

REINHOLD NIEBUHR

Reinhold Niebuhr (1892-1971) was a theologian who played a prominent role in political and social life in America during this century. In 1914 he graduated from Yale, and then he served in a church in Detroit amongst people who worked in the motor industry. This practical experience changed his thinking in many ways, and was to become crucial for his developing theology. He eventually became Professor of Applied Theology at Union Theological Seminary in New York. Reinhold had a brother, Richard, who also became an influential theologian.

Reinhold's experience amongst the workers proved to him that the optimistic ideas of liberal Protestantism about human nature and society were seriously mistaken. At the very root of life, individual and corporate, is sin, the essence of which is pride. Liberal Protestantism had attempted to do away with sin, and so had become hopeful about human achievements. Niebuhr saw the injustice that this had brought to the social and institutional levels of life, and hence spoke out against it.

Such ideas were presented in his work...

What confronted the power structures at work in society was the righteousness and transcendence of Christ. This righteousness brought justice to the workplace and to society.

Moral Man and Immoral Society

1932

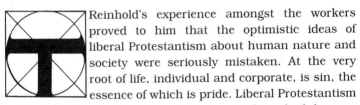

The Nature and Destiny of Man became Niebuhr's fullest expression of his theology.

1941-1943

135

Niebuhr was clearly influenced by Marxist thought, and perhaps he came close to being a Christian Marxist who denounced the evils of a society as a whole. Nevertheless, he later became highly critical of Marxism as well, and in the aftermath of World War II he became concerned with the issues of the Cold War.

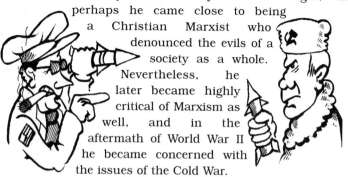

Someone who speaks out against injustice and attempts to reintroduce the seriousness of sin to Christian theology, is a theologian to take notice of. There are a number of criticisms of Niebuhr. Barth argued that he allowed the world to set his theological agenda too much. Others have argued that Niebuhr left out Christian love when trying to fight against injustice, or that he was too pessimistic about human nature.

IN SPITE OF ALL THIS, POLITICIANS AND OTHERS CONSULTED NIEBUHR ON MANY ISSUES AS HE BECAME A LEADING THEOLOGIAN WHO ATTEMPTED TO BRING HIS THEOLOGY TO BEAR ON THE WIDER ISSUES AT HAND.

PAUL TILLICH

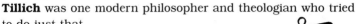

Many liberal scholars did not set out to be 'liberal'. Instead their aim was to retell the Christian faith in a way which was relevant and appropriate to the modern world. **Paul Tillich** was one modern philosopher and theologian who tried to do just that.

Paul Tillich (1886-1965) was educated in Germany, but when Hitler came to power in 1933 he moved to the United States where his career prospered. Throughout his work the thinking of various people can be seen, from the likes of **Schleiermacher** to the psychological work of **Jung**.

Tillich's most important work was his 3 volume...

Systematic Theology

1951-63

which centred on the **'method of correlation'**.

What is Tillich's method of correlation? In essence, Tillich analysed the human situation which we all find ourselves in. This situation raises a number of existential questions, that is questions about our being,

WHAT DO WE DO?

WHY ARE WE HERE?

HOW DO WE COPE?

AND SO ON..

137

If we then look at the Christian faith, theology provides us with 'symbols' which in fact provide the answers to these questions.

Symbols were important to Tillich, as theology is always in the business of using symbols to point to things which they symbolise. However, symbols are not mere pointers, they are more important than that. Symbols can also share in the thing that they point to - one often used example is that of the American flag. The flag points to the greatness of the American nation, but it also shares in it. Even more than this, Christian symbols point beyond themselves to the one who is the 'ground of their being', that is God.

Armed with the Christian symbols, the theologian provides answers to the questions the world raises, thus providing a correlation between the two.

Tillich highlighted five areas of correlation -

REASON AND REVELATION

HUMAN EXISTENCE AND CHRIST

BEING AND GOD

THE AMBIGUITIES OF LIFE AND THE SPIRIT

THE MEANING OF HISTORY AND THE KINGDOM OF GOD

138

Tillich argued that because of this method of correlation, and because of the nature of God, theology can never be final - it is always working its way towards, although it never gets to, the 'ultimate concern', who is God.

Tillich is a great example of one who tried to reformulate the faith whilst taking on all that the modern world has to offer.

However, it is arguable whether the questions he isolated from human experience are real ones, or are questions which he conveniently brings up. Even more so, are the answers that his theology provides set by the questions, rather than the other way around?

TEILHARD de CHARDIN

A French Roman Catholic theologian, **Pierre Teilhard de Chardin** was heavily influenced by Darwinian theories, and was censored for his views due to this. He saw theology in evolutionary terms, and as human beings developed out of the world, a human consciousness developed into a spiritual consciousness. All of this is drawn together in the Omega Point, that is God, and God's love which directs this evolutionary process is seen most supremely in Christ.

I'VE GOT A BANANA

I'VE GOT A SOUL

His major work... sets forth this thesis.

The Phenomenon of Man

1955

Criticisms of his work: as God becomes changing and linked with the material world, God then starts to 'disappear' and Christianity loses its identity.

139

JÜRGEN MOLTMANN

Recent modern theology has seen numerous attempts to follow in the path of past debates. However, a number of theologians have attempted to reframe doctrine in a new and imaginative way. **Moltmann**, together with **Wolfhart Pannenberg**, are just two examples of this.

Jürgen Moltmann (b.1926) served as a prisoner of war during World War II, during which time he became a Christian. In 1952 he became a pastor, and in 1967 a Professor of Systematic Theology at Tubingen. His theological reflection has initially been expressed in a trilogy of works, which has since been supplemented by a number of large works developing his framework for specific Christian doctrines.

In 1964 Moltmann published his...

Theology of Hope

1964

It's main aim is to reintroduce the notion of **eschatological hope** back into theology. Eschatological hope, the hope that comes from knowing that there is an end and a purpose for everything, is vital to theology.

Very often this hope has been lost in the church. Either we find it hard to believe what the Bible says about the end times and so we abandon it, or we say that Jesus belonged to a past era and so believed things we cannot.

On the other hand, the church has either put this hope in a timeless God that does not affect our lives in the here and now, or Christians have put their hope in church structures or supposedly Christian societies.

Moltmann says that all this is wrong. Central to Christianity is the resurrection, which intro- duces hope for a complete change in the way things are.

Such a hope urges us on to change things in this world as we find them now, to look for **orthopraxis** (the right way to do things) as well as **orthodoxy** (the right things to believe). Moltmann follows in the footsteps of some of Barth's theology, but especially Marxist thought and a particular Marxist philosopher, **Bloch**, who emphasised that human beings have an openness to the future which affects what they do now.

Moltmann's second work in the trilogy...

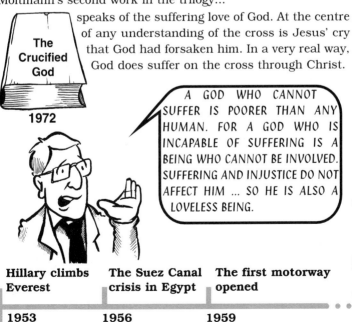

speaks of the suffering love of God. At the centre of any understanding of the cross is Jesus' cry that God had forsaken him. In a very real way, God does suffer on the cross through Christ.

The Crucified God

1972

A GOD WHO CANNOT SUFFER IS POORER THAN ANY HUMAN. FOR A GOD WHO IS INCAPABLE OF SUFFERING IS A BEING WHO CANNOT BE INVOLVED. SUFFERING AND INJUSTICE DO NOT AFFECT HIM ... SO HE IS ALSO A LOVELESS BEING.

Hillary climbs Everest

The Suez Canal crisis in Egypt

The first motorway opened

1953

1956

1959

The third work was entitled...

The Church in the Power of the Holy Spirit

1975

Moltmann has always attracted criticism, yet most theologians applaud his attempts to remain faithful to the biblical story whilst trying to be practical. Sometimes this practical emphasis has lead to him being highly critical as well, but the reintroduction of a positive eschatology into Christian theology is enormously important.

In *The Crucified God*, Moltmann speaks of God suffering. Thus he introduces the idea of divine passibility, that God can suffer, rather than impassibility. How does this relate to what we traditionally understand about God, and with the different ways in which the Bible presents God?

GOD CAN SUFFER

WOLFHART PANNENBERG

As a Protestant theologian concerned with both history and the existential encounter with Christ, **Pannenberg** (b.1928) has been an important figure in twentieth century theology. A German Lutheran, Pannenberg is best known for his concern for history, and his emphasis on eschatology.

Pannenberg has stressed the importance to theology of history. Jesus was a historical man, the revelation of God. The incarnation into flesh is necessary, otherwise theology faces a Gnostic heresy.

In contrast with Bultmann, he sees the establishment of the history of Jesus as possible and as necessary. The historical Jesus reveals the true God, and is the culmination of the plans of God.

> THUS PANNENBERG'S CHRISTOLOGY IS DONE FROM BELOW - HE CONSTRUCTS HIS VIEW OF CHRIST FROM THE HISTORICAL JESUS UPWARDS, NOT FROM THE DIVINE WORD DOWNWARDS.

The fundamental event to understanding Jesus is the resurrection, for it is this which confers on him his full status.

Into this emphasis on history, Pannenberg introduces a unique contribution. All of history finds its ultimate meaning in the end, that is, in eschatology. When God brings all things together, when the last days occur, then history will have fulfilled its own goal. This is known as **'the ontological priority of the future'**. What this means is that all of life is determined and made sense of by where it is going.

> OH, IT MAKES SENSE NOW!

Pannenberg brings together a number of important elements of modern theology. As well as being creative, he wished to stand in line with tradition. Linking theology with history is an important exercise in understanding the relationship between humanity and God.

The Beatles were founded	Radio 1 first broadcast by the BBC	The 'Troubles' start in Northern Ireland
1963	1967	1969

143

KARL RAHNER

In the modern era it has not only been Protestantism that has struggled to make the Christian faith relevant to the times. Roman Catholic theologians have also wrestled with this task, and have tried to engage with modern critical thought to bring theology into the twentieth century. Both **Karl Rahner** and **Hans Küng** are examples of such theologians.

Karl Rahner (1904-1984)became one of the most influential Roman Catholic theologians of the twentieth century, and apart from anything else he played a major role as a papal theological expert before and after the **Second Vatican Council**. Beginning as a Jesuit priest, he then taught in both Germany and Austria. Characteristic of his method was the writing of essays rather than full length books.

YUK, I HATE ESSAYS.

 During his lifetime and beyond he has become most well known for his collections of essays...

Theological Investigations

Rahner was influenced by the existentialism of **Martin Heidegger**. At the base of Rahner's theology is human experience as expressed in theological terms, that is, a **theological anthropology**.

The key to all theological questions for Rahner is human experience. However, this is not just any experience, but human life as it focuses on and points beyond towards a **transcendental experience**.

WHAT'S A TRANSCENDENTAL EXPERIENCE?

DON'T KNOW MAN!

The implication this has for his theology is that he attempts to understand traditional teachings of the church in a way that can have meaning for modern people -

WHAT'S <u>TRADITIONAL</u> MEAN?

not just any meaning, but existential meaning, meaning that impacts the lives we lead.

All human beings have the free choice to accept or reject the grace of God which is already present in human nature.

Rahner has also written much on the Trinity, the church, death, and the spiritual life. He also wrote a systematic theology...

1976

One of the most well known outworkings of this theological anthropology is Rahner's approach to **salvation**. The traditional teaching of the Roman Catholic church has been that there is no salvation outside the church.

However, Rahner teaches that the grace of God can work in a person of a non-Christian religion, or even in a person of no religion at all. For example, an atheist can encounter God through his conscience, even without knowing about God or the Christian faith.

THERE IS NO GOD!

OH YES THERE IS!

HUMANS RULE

Such a person may be saved, and his or her salvation comes only through Christ, but because God wills that all people are saved, they may be what Rahner calls **'anonymous Christians'** - Christians without knowing it. This position is known as **inclusivism**, and contrasts the more traditional position (**exclusivism**) or a more radical position (**pluralism** - that you can be saved through any religion, and that the Christian tradition has no role to play in this at all).

Rahner must be commended for his attempt to take the issue of salvation and other religions seriously. However, is he guilty of emptying Christian faith of any real element? Would an atheist or a Hindu object at being called an 'anonymous Christian'?

SECOND VATICAN COUNCIL

1962-65

The Roman Catholic church recognised the meeting of a council from 1962-1965 as the 21st ecumenical council. A major event in Roman Catholic history, Vatican II involved approximately 2300 theologians, and approved 16 major pronouncements. Its significance lay in a number of matters. It approved the use of the language of the day in worship, rather than Latin, and most significantly, it encouraged dialogue with other denominations and other religions. In its attitude to other religions, the council adopted a position similar to that of Karl Rahner, which believed that non-Christians may achieve salvation even if they had no explicit knowledge of Christ.

146

HANS KÜNG

Any theologian who can write books of 700 pages long which non-Christians end up reading is worth taking note of! Although not one of the most orthodox Roman Catholic theologians, **Hans Küng** (b.1928) is certainly one of the most widely read.

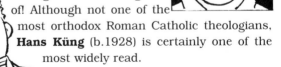

ON THE OTHER HAND MAYBE I DO LIKE ESSAYS!

Küng is a Swiss Roman Catholic who teaches in Tubingen. Much of his life has been taken up in the role of being an apologist, attempting to articulate the Christian faith in a manner which makes it relevant to modern day life. In addition he has been heavily involved in the ecumenical task, and in attempts to reform parts of the Roman Catholic Church.

Küng's first major work was on the subject of **Justification**. In an attempt to bridge the gap of 400 years of history and illustrate how close the Protestant and Roman churches actually were on the issue of justification, Küng examined the teaching of the Council of Trent and of Karl Barth on this important issue. His conclusion was that there were no irreconcilable differences between Barth and Trent. Barth actually thought Küng had done a good job, and several Roman Catholic thinkers were also impressed. Although this had only been Küng's thesis work, it was an immense contribution to the ecumenical project.

Charlie Chaplin dies	Prince Charles marries Lady Diana Spencer	The wreckage of the Titanic discovered
1977	**1981**	**1985**

His other works have been broader, with titles such as...

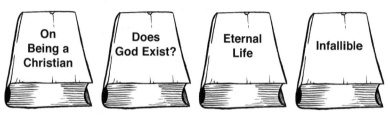

| On Being a Christian | Does God Exist? | Eternal Life | Infallible |

The work on what it means to be a Christian was widely read as an apologetic work. The works dealing with the church and the question of **infallibility** were more controversial. His argument was that no human or human organisation can claim to be without error - not even the pope or the church. Such a questioning attitude lead to Küng being asked to step down from his role as an official Roman Catholic theologian in 1979. In the light of this Küng received much public support, and continued to teach at Tubingen in another capacity.

 Küng's work can in a sense be seen as an attempt to build bridges - between Protestants and Roman Catholics, between Christians and society at large, and between the authority of the church and the normal Christian in the pew.

He has since turned his eyes to issues such as other religions and how they relate to the Christian faith, and what Christians have to say in the face of the huge environmental pressures our planet faces.

Live Aid Concert raises £40 million for famine victims in Ethiopia

1985

WORLD COUNCIL OF CHURCHES

1948

An important development in 20th century church relations, the World Council of Churches was established in 1948 after a number of meetings earlier in the century which suggested this may be possible. In 1983, 301 church denominations were involved. The council not only promotes relationships between denominations, but in 1982 reached a theological consensus on Baptism, Eucharist and Ministry. The Council is defined as "a fellowship of churches which accept the Lord Jesus Christ as Lord and Saviour". As this was a limited theological definition, entries were added on Scripture and Trinity. The Council expresses a Christian concern for unity, a desire in any ecclesiology. However, the question remains as to whether unity is achieved at the expense of truth.

LIBERATION THEOLOGY

Another significant theological movement in the 20th century was **liberation theology**, arising in the late 1960s, predominantly in Latin America. The question posed is this: What does theology have to say to the vast majority of the world who are oppressed and poor? Most of theology has been done by the powerful and by the rich. Does theology therefore have anything to say to the rest of the world?

Therefore, instead of the usual discussions of Western theology, examining for example the Trinity, or church government, liberation theology wanted to ask questions about God's justice.

149

God has in fact identified with the poor and become involved, on the cross of Jesus. There God suffers all that the oppressed have suffered. Whereas traditional theology often started from God and revelation, liberation theology saw the poor and the oppressed as its starting point. **Leonardo Boff** and **Gustavo Gutiérrez** are examples of liberation theologians.

Liberation theology has not been confined to Latin America, and has been thought through in black cultures, in contexts such as South Africa, and in groups where oppression has many faces. For example, womanist theology combines the concerns of liberation theology for blacks with feminist theology.

In general, liberation theology has attempted to offer hope, drawing on the work of **Moltmann**, and certain Marxist ideas. **Vatican II** was quite influenced by liberation theology.

Perhaps the key story for liberationists is that of the Exodus, explaining how God led his people out of suffering, and becoming a story that can inspire and teach all oppressed groups.

FEMINIST THEOLOGY

A read through this book will reveal one startling fact about theology - most of it has been done by men.

Feminist theology arose in the twentieth century, partly as a reaction to this fact. Christian theology seems to have a male God, a male Bible, a male Saviour, and a male Church lead by male preachers and male theologians. Where is the place for women?

> ## HEY IT'S A MAN THING!

Feminist theology therefore tackles such issues. It is not a unified movement, and can range from liberal to evangelical, and from liberation to post-Christian feminist theology. A key issue is that of hermeneutics, of how to study and interpret the Bible. Is the Bible **patriarchal** (emphasising men as above women), does it give any positive images of women, does it speak to women of today, etc.?

Feminist theologians include **Mary Daly, Elisabeth Schussler Fiorenza**, **Rosemary Radford Ruether**, and **Phyllis Trible**. The issues are central to Christian theology. For example, when we refer to God as "He", do we mean that God is essentially male, or is this the way in which God has chosen to be revealed? Is it permissible to refer to God as "she"...

> ## WHAT NO BEARD?

and if Christ identified with what it means to be a human, does this include genuine female experience? The church has had a bad record in oppressing women, and theologians have been called to reflect and act on this.

153

EVANGELICALISM

As theology enters a new century, a number of influential movements (rather than people) can be identified.

Evangelicalism is a movement amongst churches and theology. Protestant in nature, it emerged as a reaction to liberal theology, and evangelicals strive to maintain orthodoxy within and outside traditional denominational structures.

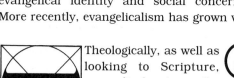

Evangelicals look back to the creeds, to the Reformation, to Puritans, and to certain revival movements in the 18th and 19th centuries.

> ABOVE ALL, EVANGELICALS LOOK BACK TO SCRIPTURE AS THE FIRST AND FINAL COURT OF AUTHORITY IN ALL MATTERS OF THEOLOGY.

Evangelicalism saw great growth in the 19th century, with a resurgence of both evangelical identity and social concern. More recently, evangelicalism has grown world-wide.

Theologically, as well as looking to Scripture, evangelicals stress the need for conversion, the need to evangelise, the importance of substitutionary atonement, and the second coming of Christ.

Some notable contemporary evangelical theologians include **John Stott** and **Carl Henry**.

POSTMODERNISM

More a philosophy than a theology, **postmodernism** is now recognised to be something which affects all of life and thought. The difficulty is in defining postmodernism. Its name suggests it comes after in terms of time and thought everything which is....

LIKE ME!

I REASON THAT REASON HAS ALL THE ANSWERS!

Modernism is characterised by confidence in the power of reason, optimism concerning human progress and ability, and the fact that one philosophical account explains all there is. Postmodernism, denies that reason can solve all our problems and come to one solution.

I REASON THAT REASON CAN'T TELL US ANYTHING... ER.

IT DOES NOT BELIEVE THAT THERE IS ONE BIG STORY (A META-NARRATIVE) WHICH EXPLAINS EVERYTHING, OR THAT HUMANITY IS NECESSARILY GETTING BETTER.

For theology, postmodernism questions whether it is possible to know any absolutes at all (**relativism**), and argues that there are many ways of understanding the world which may be equally valid (**pluralism**). Postmodern theologians may be extremely sceptical about the reality of God, and of talking about God (**Don Cuppitt**, **Mark Taylor**), or they may be cautiously optimistic about answering theological questions, even if we may not know the whole truth.

The difficulty with postmodernism is that it takes so many forms, and that we are currently living in the midst of it. Perhaps in 20 years analysis and implications may be easier to see.

153

AS THEOLOGY ENTERS THE TWENTY FIRST CENTURY, THE JOURNEY TO UNDERSTAND GOD AND THE WORLD CONTINUES. THE MODERN AND POSTMODERN PERIOD CHALLENGES MUCH OF WHAT HAS GONE BEFORE, BUT ALSO HOPES TO BUILD ON IT.

QUESTIONS THAT FACE THEOLOGY INCLUDE THE QUESTION OF HOW OTHER RELIGIONS ARE UNDERSTOOD, THE ROLE OF WOMEN IN THEOLOGY AND THE CHURCH, THE NATURE OF TRUTH, AND MANY MORE.

AS WORLD-WIDE MOVEMENTS SUCH AS EVANGELICALISM BECOME STRONGER,

PERHAPS THEOLOGY IS TURNING AGAIN TO ITS ROOTS.

WHETHER THIS WILL BE THE CASE REMAINS TO BE SEEN.

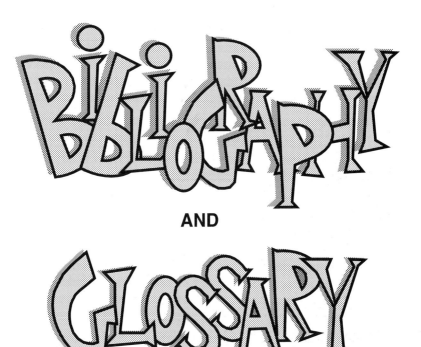

BIBLIOGRAPHY

AND

GLOSSARY

THESE ARE ONLY A SMALL SELECTION OF WORKS AVAILABLE. THEY WILL IN TURN POINT IN FURTHER DIRECTIONS, SO KEEP DIGGING!

New Dictionary of Theology

Sinclair Ferguson and David Wright, Eds (Leicester: IVP, 1988)
An invaluable reference tool for all students of theology, with helpful bibliographies to follow up ideas.

The Modern Theologians

David Ford, Editor (Oxford: Blackwell, 1997)
All the main theologians and movements of the twentieth century are introduced and discussed at an undergraduate level.

Early Christian Doctrines

J N D Kelly (London: A & C Black, 1977)
The key text on Patristic theology, and vital for all that follows.

The Lion Book of Christian Thought

Tony Lane (Oxford: Lion, 1984)
A brilliant condensed and well detailed step up from this potted guide. Includes sections of important texts.

**Alister E McGrath
(Oxford: Blackwell, 1997 - 2nd Edition)**
One of the best introductions to Christian theology available. A great next step, together with the companion volume...

**Alister E McGrath, Editor
(Oxford: Blackwell, 1995)**

**Alister E McGrath
(Oxford: Blackwell, 1993)**
Helpful outline of what went into and came out of the Reformation.

**Mark A Noll
(Leicester: Apollos, 1998)**
A lively and well informed introduction to historical events of theological importance. Good for 6th form / 1st year undergraduate level.

**Tim Dowley, Editor
(Oxford: Lion, 1990)**
Beautifully illustrated and detailed history. Great reference tool.

Adiaphora - applied to matters of disagreement over theology which are deemed to be of little consequence

Anabaptists - the radical extreme wing of the Reformation, emphasising the need for adult believer baptism

Analogy - a method of explaining something by comparing it with something else

Anthropology - discussion of what it means to be human

Antiochenes - Western Christians in Patristic period who emphasised the oneness in God

Apokatastasis - universalism, the belief that everyone and everything will be saved

Apollinarianism - belief that Jesus did not have a human soul

Apologists - those who attempt to explain Christianity to an unbelieving audience

Arianism - heresy named after Arius which taught that the Son is not divine as the Father is

Aristotle - Greek philosopher who influenced many theologiansa

Ascetism - the withdrawal of the church from the world and its trappings

Atonement - what happened when Jesus died, and the understanding of how this dealt with sin

Baptism - ritual involving water to initiate someone into the Christian faith

Baptist - denomination which stress independent church government, and believer's baptism

Bible - Scripture, God's Word - the book which Christians accept as authoritive, consisting of Old Testament (the Hebrew Bible also recognised by Jews) and the New Testament

Book of Common Prayer - Anglican book setting out church order, theology, services,etc.

Canon - the rule, that is the extent of the Bible - that which is accepted to be in the Bible, excluding other books which do not have the same authority

Christology - discussion concerning the nature, person, and work of Christ

Communion - see Eucharist

Confession - a statement of Christian doctrines

Confirmation - ritual to confirm someone who has already been baptised

Correlation - Paul Tillich's method of bringing the world and Scripture together

Creation ex nihilo - the belief that God created the world and the universe out of nothing

Creed - a list of Christian beliefs

Demythologisation - Bultmann's programme of reading the kerygma out of the New Testament

Depravity - the utter fallenness of humanity

Dialectic - method of arguing which opposes negatives in order to come to a conclusion

Donatists - group which believed that only the saved could be part of church

Ecclesiology - discussion of the nature, authority, structure and government of the church

Economy of Salvation - how God reveals himself in his plan of salvation, as Father, then as Son, and then as Holy Spirit

Ecumenical - something which aims to bring churches of different denominations together

Ecumenical Council - a meeting of all church parties to resolve a doctrinal debate, e.g. Nicaea in 325

Elect - those whom God has decided, or whom God knows in advance, that will be saved

Enlightenment - period of history from the 18th century onwards which is characterised by science, reason, progress, etc., in all areas of human life

Eschatology - discussion of the future, the end of the world, the second coming of Christ, the last things

Eucharist, Mass, Lord's Supper, Holy Communion - sacrament instituted by Jesus to remember his death, variously interpreted

Exclusivism - the belief that only Christians will be saved

Excommunication - the process of removing someone from the church due to heresy or wrong practice

Existentionalism - philosophy that emphasises experi-

ence and the importance of encountering the truth
Experience - events in life which are used to form a theology

Faith - belief and trust; or, the description of set of beliefs
Fall - event that happened after creation, whereby Adam and Eve rebel against God
Filioque Controversy - did the Spirit proceed from the Father alone, or from both the Father and the Son
Foreknowledge - God's knowledge of what happens before it does happen
Free will - the ability of human beings to choose what to do

Gnosticism - a movement which emphasised the importance of knowledge, and dualism between the material and spiritual worlds
God - in Christian theology, God is one and three - the creator and sustainer of the universe; the subject of Christian theology
Gospel - good news, the message of Christianity; or, one of the four gospels in the New Testament
Grace - God's unconditional love

Hermeneutics - the practice and method of interpreting, especially Scripture
Holy Spirit - The third person of the Trinity
Homoousios - term used to mean that the Son is of one substance with the Father
Humanist - in the Reformation, someone who argued for a return to the original sources for theology and philosophy; in modern period, someone who makes a decision on the basis of good for other humans and humanity in general, rather than any other philosophy
Hypostases - term used to identify the three beings in the Godhead

Icons - images that represent Christ in a picture
Immaculate Conception - the belief that Mary was born without sin, because she gave birth to Jesus who was also sinless

Immortal - not being subject to death, living forever
Incarnation - belief that God became human in the person of Christ
Inclusivism - the belief that although others can be saved through Christ, others from other religions may be saved through Christ without knowing it
Indulgences - sold to Christians to release them from some of the punishment awaiting them after death
Infallible - belief that a thing cannot make a mistake - applied by Catholics to the Pope, by some Protestants to the Bible
Inspiration - that the writing of the Bible was inspired, that is directed and guided, by God

Jesus - man who lived in Palestine, described in the New Testament, and believed to be the second person of the Trinity
Justification - the process of being made righteous before God

Kerygma - the essential message of the gospel which humans have to respond to
Liberalism - movement of theology which interprets the historic creeds in an attempt to present Christianity to the modern world
Limited atonement - belief that the effects of the cross are only applicable to the elect
Logos - the word, the principal behind the world: in John's Gospel, the Logos becomes human
Logos spermatikos - the seed of the Logos in all human beings
Lollards - followers of John Wycliffe
Lord's supper, see Eucharist

Macedonians - heretics who denied the deity of the Holy Spirit
Manichaeism - Gnostic religious belief
Marcion - heretic who disregarded the Old Testament and much of the New Testament
Martyr - someone who dies for their faith
Mass, see Eucharist
Methodists - denomination formed following Wesley

Mission - the act of bringing Christianity to people who have never heard it before

Monarchians - heretics who believed there are no distinctions in the Godhead

Monasticism - the concentration of church life and thought in monasteries

Monophysitism - belief that Christ only has one nature, divine nature

Mysticism - a religious approach which emphasises the mysterious, contemplative aspects of religious life

Natural theology - the attempt to learn about God from what we can see around us, and from reason

Neo-orthodox - description given to the likes of Barth who reacted against liberalism, but in a novel way

Nestorianism - named after Nestorius, emphasising the separateness of the two natures in Christ

Nominalism - philosophy that believes that universals do not actually exist, opposed to realism

Omnipotent - having power to do anything

Ontological argument - argument for the existence of God based on reason

Original Sin - Adam and Eve's first sin, which has contaminated all human beings, making none sinless

Orthodoxy - literally, right belief, usually accepted as represented by certain creeds or confessions

Orthopraxy - right actions, as opposed to orthodoxy

Pelagianism - heresy named after Pelagius, emphasising freewill

Pentateuch - the first five books of the Old Testament

Perfectionism - belief that Christians can become perfect before they get to heaven

Philosophy - thoughts about the world, about life, about the nature of things

Pilgrimage - a journey with a religious aim, perhaps visiting a holy city or burial ground

Plato - Greek philosopher who influenced many theologians

Platonism - philosophy following Plato

Pluralism - with regard to religion, the belief that all

religions lead the same way, all religions offer salvation
Predestination - belief that a person's destiny is decided by God before creation
Protestantism - those who protested against the Roman Catholic church, now a general term to describe whole churches

Q - a hypothetical source behind the synoptic gospels (Matthew, Mark, and Luke)
Quaker - denomination begun after George Fox, emphasising religious experience

Realism - philosophy which believes that universals do in actual fact exist
Reason - the use of our minds
Redeemer - the one who saves, in Christianity, Jesus
Redemption - salvation, setting free
Reformed Theology - theology that follows the great Protestant reformers. It can refer to Protestant theology in general, or a distinction can be made between Lutheran and Reformed (Calvinistic) theology
Resurrection - belief that Christ rose from the dead
Revelation - God revealing something of himself to humans, rather than humans deciding what God is like by reason
Revival - a religious event where great numbers of people are converted and drastic changes occur in society
Roman Catholic Church - church which takes its authority from the Pope in Rome

Sacraments - rituals used in a church to communicate something of God's grace - interpretations of how and why differ
Scholasticism - theological approach emphasising reason and system
Sin - both the individual acts and the condition which affects all humans, doing what is against God's will
Son of Man - a New Testament term used to refer to Jesus
Soteriology - discussion of how and what it means to be saved
Soul - part of the human person believed to continue

163

after death

Spirituality - a person's religious attitude and life

Stigmata - the signs of Christ's crucifixion in his hands and feet

Subordination - putting someone or something under the authority of another, making them a second order

Substitution - the idea that at the atonement Christ was substituted for humanity

Synoptics - the three gospels that appear to be most alike (Matthew, Mark, and Luke), leaving John aside

Theotokos - mother of God

Thomists - those who follow the theology of Thomas Aquinas

Transubstantiation - the belief that during the Eucharist, the bread is transformed into Christ's body, and the wine into Christ's blood

Trinity - the doctrine of God which believes in one God, three persons

Tritheism - belief that there are three equal Gods

Universals - concepts for a whole category, such as dogs, tables etc.

Vulgate - the Latin translation of the Bible

Will - a person's desires and ability to decide

Word - see Bible; or, the Logos